NINE HUNDRED
PRIMARY SCHOOL
TEACHERS

Nottinghamshire Primary School Research Project

Nine Hundred Primary School Teachers

Michael Bassey

with a Foreword by Lady Plowden

NFER Publishing Company Ltd.

Published by the NFER Publishing Company Ltd.,
Darville House, 2 Oxford Road East,
Windsor, Berks. SL4 1DF
Registered Office: The Mere, Upton Park, Slough, Berks, SL1 2DQ
First published 1978
© Michael Bassey, 1978
ISBN 0 85633 157 0

Typeset by Yale Press Limited,
Carmichael Road, Norwood, London SE25
Printed in Great Britain by
Whitefriars Press, Tonbridge Kent
Distributed in the USA by Humanities Press Inc.,
Atlantic Highlands, New Jersey 07716 USA.

Contents

FOREWORD

This most comprehensive report on the practices of primary education in Nottinghamshire gives a great deal of information about the day by day work of a large number of teachers. It is written in a way which should be readily intelligible to other teachers. I found it of enormous interest, particularly since Dr. Bassey has attempted no judgments of the teachers' replies, these are left to the reader.

Judging from the replies, there does not seem to be any danger of the schools in Nottinghamshire moving into the so-called 'progressive methods' in which 'children do as they please'. Table 5 shows this well, in the answers to 'How does a typical pupil spend the 27½ hours of a typical week?' I believe that a national survey would similarly show that throughout the country teachers are in general responsibly structuring children's experience in the classroom.

I was somewhat depressed by Tables 33 and 79, because many children are not able to take their school work home. This would seem to militate against the attempts which are being made, as described in Table 100, to involve parents in their children's school experience. On the other hand, it is pleasing to see in Tables 51 and 101 how many parents are providing regular assistance in these schools. Times change, for I remember the outcry in 1967 at the suggestion that there might be teachers' aides.

My overall impression from the report is of the variety of practice in these schools, of the lack of gimmicky 'progressive' methods and of the care taken in covering areas of the curriculum; but sadly there does seem to be a lack of planned progession either in class or in school.

This report should be of interest to teachers and to others directly concerned with primary education. Written about Nottinghamshire teachers, it will be of equal interest to teachers in all parts of the country. Similar studies could be carried out in many of these with advantage.

Bridget Plowden

PREAMBLE

Few teachers know how other teachers teach. Each teacher develops ways of organizing her class more or less on her own and with little opportunity for knowing how other teachers carry out the same tasks. This is not a research finding, but a viewpoint; it was the starting point for the research reported here.

The aim of the Project was to find out how teachers in one geographic area organize the day-to-day work of their pupils; we set out to describe the major practices of primary school teachers in part of Nottinghamshire. The method of enquiry was to interview teachers with a schedule of questions.

How many teachers work individually with classes of their own and how many work in teams? How many work in classrooms or in open plan spaces? Are the children age-grouped or vertically-grouped? How much time do they spend on classwork, groupwork, and individual work? How much time do they spend on different subjects; what subjects are taught? What approaches do teachers use in teaching mathematics, reading, writing, spoken language, physical education, music, art and craft, and topic work? What text books are used; what stories are read; what radio and television programmes are used; what visitors come into the classroom to work with the children; what visits are made? What tests are used; how much written work is marked; when is it marked; what records are kept; what ultimately happens to the children's work - do they take it home? Are there regular playtimes; what do teachers do during assembly? How far do headteachers influence their staffs? Who decides on outline syllabuses? What responsibilities do headteachers delegate? What are the arrangements for transfer from infant school to junior school and from primary school to secondary school? What are the links between home and school; what organization for parents exists; how many parents give voluntary help in school; what do parents do in school? These are some of the questions to which we sought answers.

In the autumn of 1976 many newly qualified teachers were without teaching posts. At Trent Polytechnic, we sponsored a Job Creation Programme, financed by the Manpower Services Commission, through which 25 former students of the Polytechnic, and subsequently others, joined me to form the Nottinghamshire Primary Schools Research Project team. These people were on the waiting list of the Nottinghamshire Education Department for primary school teaching appointments and during the year most of them left the Project to take up posts in schools.

We interviewed 893 teachers in 114 Nottinghamshire primary schools and asked our questions. This report collates the information which these teachers gave about the ways in which they organize their teaching. It is a descriptive report, not an evaluative one; there is no attempt to show that one procedure is better than another. Apart from my personal view that the quest for universal 'best methods' is an impossible search for phantoms, it was clear that the research officers were too inexperienced to attempt any kind of evaluation, but that they could use their training to conduct structured interviews through which the work of teachers could be described.

The Project was only possible because of the goodwill of a large number of people: officers and advisers of the Nottinghamshire Education Department; administrative and computer staff of the Polytechnic; tutors in the Polytechnic School of Education; librarians of the Polytechnic and of the Nottinghamshire County Library; the local branches of the

National Association of Headteachers, the National Association of Schoolmasters and the Union of Women Teachers,
and the National Union of Teachers; and, in particular, the
teachers whom we interviewed. My hope is that these people,
and the 31 research officers who worked with me, will feel
that this report justifies their efforts.

In an earlier paragraph I have expressed my view that there
are no universal 'best methods' in teaching. For a particular
teacher with a particular class working in a particular
teaching space at a particular time, one method of organization or one topic or one story, etc., may be best. For the
same teacher with another class, or in another teaching space
or at another time, something different may be best. The
decision as to what is the most appropriate method or topic
or story usually lies with the individual teacher; her excel-
lence at making such decisions depends in part upon the
extent to which she is aware of the options open to her.

The purpose of the Project lies in this report. If it is true
that 'few teachers know how other teachers teach' then my
hope is that the report will help make teachers more aware
of the variety of practices in common use and so widen the
base from which their classroom decisions are made.
Changing one's teaching methods over the years is an important contribution to success in teaching, because each
change provides a new stimulus to thought and to enthu-
siasm.

The report should also be of consequence to those who
train primary school teachers, for it provides a powerful
reminder that there is a great gap between the job requirements of primary school teachers and the college training
which many receive. Primary school teaching is very deman-
ding of professional knowledge, skills and values; in the BEd.
and Cert. Ed. courses too little time is usually spent on these
attributes, and too much time on academic matters that may
be interesting but less relevant to teaching. There is one other
way in which the report could be of consequence. It contains
many pointers to further educational research and in-service

development. Specialists may feel that a teaching method which is revealed to be popular could be modified to achieve better learning, or that certain books that are widely used should be superseded by others. People looking for worthwhile research projects may decide to follow up the findings on organizational patterns, on teaching methods, on children with special needs, on the use of TV and radio in school, or on record keeping, for example.

The report is in four parts: I describes the research procedures; II gives the results of interviews with junior teachers and III the results from infant teachers; IV collates the replies from headteachers.

Educational research is often denigrated by teachers on the grounds that, when reported, it either tells of things in incomprehensible language, or it tells of things that teachers feel are already known. If the reader feels that the former is the case in this report, then I have failed by not writing in sufficiently clear and simple ways; but if the reader criticizes the report on the grounds that what is written here is already known, I am prepared to stick my neck out and quarrel. The intention is not simply to report on the results of 893 interviews; it is to present the results in such a way that they help the teacher reading them to think deeply about her own teaching in relation to the variety of ways in which her fellow teachers conduct their classes. In this way I hope the report will serve the end to which I believe all educational research should be directed - towards the improvement of education.

PART 1 RESEARCH PROCEDURES

This survey is based on 49 per cent of the 232 primary (JMI), infant and junior schools in the Nottinghamshire districts of Nottingham, Gedling and Newark. In all 893 teachers were interviewed in the period from October, 1976 to March, 1977.

This part of the report describes how the data on these teachers was collected. It indicates the extent to which the teachers interviewed are representative of the whole area. It also discusses some features of the presentation of the data.

Three questionnaires for use in interviews were drawn up. The questions were initially compiled with the assistance of a number of Polytechnic tutors, and then refined through a series of discussions with the research team of newly qualified teachers, with local authority advisers, and with the members of the Project's Advisory Committee. This Advisory Committee consisted of three teachers, representing the NAHT, the NAS/UWT and the NUT, three senior members of the Nottinghamshire Education Department, and three members of the Polytechnic. The questionnaires were then tested in a group of 10 schools and subsequently revised.

The essential criterion for a question to be included in the survey was that the collated answers would be of interest to primary school teachers. It was also important, of course, that the questions be unambiguous, suitable for brief answers, and that the answers be suitable for collation. The number of questions was limited to what could be covered in about an hour of interview.

The schools in the area were advised by the Nottinghamshire Education Department that they were likely to be approached by the research team and a series of five briefing meetings for headteachers were held to discuss the Project and to describe the intended procedures. At these meetings it was stressed that participation was voluntary and that the replies of individual teachers would be confidential and not identifiable in the report. It was also stressed that the survey was to be descriptive and not evaluative; the point was made that there was no intention of trying to show that one pattern of organization or teaching method is better than another.

Of all the schools in the area, 69 per cent were invited, by letter and telephone, to participate. Of these invited schools 76 per cent agreed to be visited. In the schools visited, 86 per cent of the class teaching and team teaching teachers agreed to be interviewed.

Originally it was planned to invite all of the 232 schools in the area to participate, but since the research team was halved at Christmas, by people taking up teaching appointments, it was not possible to do this. Table A compares the schools in the survey with all of the schools in the area, and shows that the survey is somewhat over-representative of large schools, junior schools, county rather than voluntary schools and Nottingham schools. Table B compares the teachers in the survey with all of the teachers in the area.

If the purpose of the Project had been to draw generalizations about schools, for example relating size of school to pattern of organization, the skewed sampling might have weakened the validity of the conclusions. But, as explained in the Preamble, this was not the intention. The aim of the Project is to describe some of the practices of primary education in local schools. The exact values of the figures cited for different ways of working are not important. What does matter is that the number of teachers interviewed is sufficient to show the variety of ways in which the business of teaching in primary schools is conducted, and to give some indication of the relative popularity of these ways of working. I believe that this purpose has been adequately served by the 893 interviews collated in the report.

Table A   *The Schools in the Survey Compared to all the Schools in the Area*

'schools in the survey': each figure shows the percentage of schools in the area, of the category shown, surveyed. Thus, of the schools with 201 to 300 children, 55 per cent were surveyed.

'distribution in the area': these columns show the percentages of each category in the area. Thus, 32 per cent of the schools in Nottingham, Gedling and Newark contain 201 to 300 children

		schools in the survey	distribution in the area
total area		49%	
size	up to 200 children	38%	38%
	201 — 300 children	55%	32%
	301 — 400 children	63%	18%
	401 plus children	81%	12%
			100%
district	Nottingham	73%	51%
	Gedling	38%	21%
	Newark	26%	28%
			100%
type	primary	44%	45%
	infant	44%	29%
	junior	77%	26%
			100%
control	voluntary	32%	21%
	county	58%	79%
			100%

N = 232 schools in the area. Uniform sampling would require '49%' for each item in the left hand column

Table B   *The Teachers in the Survey Compared to all the Teachers in the Area*

'teachers in the survey': each figure shows the percentage of teachers in the area, of the category shown, who were interviewed. Thus, of junior teachers, 47 per cent were interviewed.

'distribution in the area': these columns show the percentages of each category in the area. Thus 50 per cent of the teachers in Nottingham, Gedling and Newark are teachers of junior children

		teachers in the survey	distribution in the area
total area		42%	
district	Nottingham	52%	61%
	Gedling	36%	19%
	Newark	21%	20%
			100%
type	headteacher	49%	11%
	junior teacher	47%	50%
	infant teacher	35%	39%
			100%

N = 2111 teachers in the area. Uniform sampling would require '42%' for each item in the left hand column.

Participation in the Project was voluntary. Headteachers were free to decline to have research officers visit their schools. In the schools which were visited, individual teachers were free to decline to be interviewed. In the individual interview, the teacher was free to decline to answer some of the questions. Methodologically this could be damaging to the sample, but ethically it was right. In the event few schools and teachers declined, and few questions were avoided. Most of the schools who declined offered unsolicited explanations - school in the throes of re-organization, acting head very busy because of double duties, etc. In 62 per cent of the schools visited, all of the teachers were interviewed.

It was also considered to be important that each person interviewed checked what the research officer had recorded. On the front page of each questionnaire used in the interviews a box had to be ticked showing that the teacher gave her approval to the report of her interview.

Confidentiality was carefully safeguarded. No names of either teachers or schools were entered on the questionnaires, nor entered on the computer record. No interview record was shown to other teachers. Only members of the research team had access to the individual data. Teachers were assured that shortly after the Project was completed the list of participants would be destroyed.

One of the obvious difficulties of trying to interview teachers at one hour per interview is that primary school teachers have no 'free periods'. This was neatly overcome in many schools by a procedure which also gave considerable satisfaction to the research officers. They visited schools in pairs and made arrangements such that one research officer interviewed a teacher while the other one took the teacher's place in the classroom.

The usual procedure was for a pair of research officers to visit a school, following a telephone appointment, and to make arrangements for interviews during the next few days. Questionnaires were given to the participating teachers to read through prior to the actual interview; this meant that the teachers were aware of what they were to be asked, and had had an opportunity to think about their answers.

Some of the questions entailed putting ticks in boxes, others required written responses which the research officer entered on the questionnaire form. A number of the questions were concerned with the amount of time which a Teacher spends on particular activities. After trying out several approaches, we settled for the five point scale using the terms 'nearly all of the time', 'most of the time', 'some of the time', 'a little of the time' 'and none of the time'. Clearly the decision to put a tick in a particular box on such a scale entails the respondent making a personal judgment about the meaning of the terms. Possible variations in the judgment of different teachers were accepted as a limitation of this type of question.

Another limitation on the validity of the data is the unknown extent to which respondents give not so much the answer which comes closest to their actual practice but the answer which they think others might see as the 'right' one. In reading the report the reader must realize that inevitably what is seen is not an exact image of what happens in the classroom, but an image which has been distorted by the process of its collection. I believe that in general the respondents have given accurate descriptions of their practice, but this belief is a matter of personal conviction rather than of empirical fact.

Research is only useful if its findings are communicated. A vast amount of data was collected in the interviews and so the report is necessarily a heavy meal for the reader. In writing the report particular attention has been paid to the presentation of the tables, in trying to make them easily intelligible. In consequence the footnotes to the tables may seem to some to be pedantic. Usually the five point scale of questioning has been narrowed to a three point scale for the presentation of the answers; this aids understanding. Parts II and III, referring respectively to junior teachers and to infant teachers, have been written in more or less the same format, but the reader who wishes to draw comparisons between these two groups has been left to do this for himself. To reiterate a point made in the Preamble, the hope is that the report will help to make teachers more aware of the variety of practices in common use and so widen the base from which their classroom decisions are made.

PART II JUNIOR TEACHERS

Introduction

In total 498 junior teachers were interviewed. These were all teachers with registration groups; 'floating' teachers and part-time teachers were not interviewed. Also probationary teachers were excluded. Of these 498 teachers, 72 per cent taught in Nottingham, 19 per cent in Gedling and 9 per cent in Newark. The following table shows the extent to which we sampled all of the teachers in each area.

Table 1   *Percentages of Junior Teachers in Each Area Interviewed*

	Nottingham	Gedling	Newark	Nottingham, Gedling and Newark combined
percentage of all the junior teachers in the area who were interviewed	55%	44%	22%	47%

Through the report 'junior' means children aged 7 to 11 and 'primary' means children aged 5 to 11. In types of school, 64 per cent of the junior teachers interviewed were in junior schools and 36 per cent in primary schools.

In terms of buildings, 80 per cent of the teachers worked in classrooms, 2 per cent in open plan areas and 18 per cent in 'semi-open spaces'; the latter term implying a classroom area plus an adjacent space which is usually shared with other classes.

The four age groups of junior children were equally represented in the interviews. Teachers were asked, 'What is the age range of most of the children taught by you most of the time: 1st year, 2nd year, 3rd year, 4th year?' They could tick as many of these as seemed appropriate. The responses show that 62 per cent were teaching mainly one age group, 35 per cent two age groups and only 2 per cent were teaching three age groups or the full range of four age groups (and these were mainly small rural schools). Teachers working with infants plus first year juniors are treated in the Report as infant teachers; they would amount to 1 per cent of the total number of junior teachers if included with them.

Nearly everybody worked mainly as a class teacher: 94 per cent. The rest consisted of 3 per cent working in pairs and 3 per cent working in teams of either three or four teachers.

We asked how many children each teacher had on her register. (In a pair or team situation the total number of children was divided by the number of teachers). Table 2 gives the findings.

Table 2 *Sizes of Classes*

number of children in the class	up to 14	15-19	20-24	25-29	30-34	35-39	40+
percentage of teachers working with each size of class	1%	1%	7%	29%	45%	16%	1%

N = 498 junior teachers. The row totals to 100%

The next section of the Report deals with timetables, with the use of time for different parts of the curriculum, and with some of the ways in which teaching is organized.

Timetables and the Use of Time

We asked teachers to enter on a Monday to Friday table the activities and subjects of a normal week for their classes. Only 2 per cent felt that their programme was so varied that it was not possible to give a timetable. The number of curriculum items in the timetables varied: 60 per cent had eight or more curriculum activities or subjects in the week, 29 per cent had six or seven, 9 per cent had five or fewer. Assembly and playtime are excluded from this listing. The request for a timetable sought answers in the terms used by teachers themselves to describe the work of a school week. But in order to be able to collate data about the time spent on different subjects and activities we had to ask a more structured question.

We posed the question 'How does a typical pupil spend the 27½ hours of a typical week?' The answers were collected in a rather complicated table which analyzed time spent in terms of both activity and teaching method. Many teachers found this question difficult to answer; as an item in a postal questionnaire it would have been useless, but, guided by the research officers, most teachers were able to give the information requested in their interview.

First, three general items of activity were defined as follows:

Assembly   When two or more classes are gathered together for communal purposes — religious observance, singing, notices, class presentations, etc.

Administration   Registration, class notices, dinner money, savings, etc.

Playtimes   'If you don't have regular playtime periods, record the time which you expect will be spent by a typical child in informal play'.

More than 90 per cent of the teachers replied in these

terms and these replies are collated in Table 3.

Table 3   *'How Does a Typical Pupil Spend the 27½ Hours of a Typical Week?' Answers for Assembly, Administration and Playtimes*

each line shows the percentages of teachers giving answers:	0 hours per week	¼-1 hour per week	1¼-2 hours per week	2¼-3 hours per week	3¼-4 hours per week	no answer
assembly	0%	6%	55%	29%	3%	7%
administration	4%	60%	27%	0%	0%	9%
playtimes	0%	1%	15%	75%*	3%	6%

N = 498 junior teachers. Horizontal rows total to 100%.
*67% of the teachers gave the figure of 2½ hours for playtimes, ie ¼ hour of each morning and each afternoon of every day

Second, seven curriculum subjects were defined. These were presumed to be sufficient to embrace any and every subject and activity occurring in the schools and, through the agency of explanations given by the research officers, seem to have made a successful net for catching the work of junior schools. The seven subjects and their definitions are:

Mathematics   This includes any activity where the *main aim is to develop mathematical concepts and skills:* instruction, work cards, exercises, practical mathematics, mental arithmetic, table recitation etc.

Language   This includes any activity where the *main aim is to promote language skills i.e.* reading aloud, reading silently, comprehension, writing, talking, listening, spelling, grammar, punctuation, handwriting, creative writing etc.

Thematic Studies   This includes study of any subjects/topics/projects on scientific, geographic, environmental, historical or Biblical

| | themes carried out individually, in groups or as a class, where the *main aims are to experience the subject matter and/ or to develop the skills of enquiry.* |

Art and Craft   This includes art, handicraft, needlework, etc. where the *main aims are to promote non-verbal imagination and expression or manual skills which facilitate creative expression.*

Music   This includes making and listening to music, singing etc.

Physical Education   This includes all the activities such as apparatus work, movement, out-of-door activities, swimming and games, where the *main aims are to promote the physical co-ordination of the body, body awareness and the acquisition of social and physical skills.*

Integrated Studies   This term implies that several aspects of the curriculum originate from a common centre of interest or topic etc.

'Integrated Studies' was included reluctantly. We recognized that many teachers try to integrate the various elements of their day-by-day curriculum, but we wanted to be able to see the school experience of children in terms of their opportunities for learning mathematics, art and craft, music etc. In collecting data the research officers only used the term 'integrated studies' where the teacher was unwilling to subdivide the activities of her class into the separate headings. This needs to be borne in mind when considering the replies tabulated in Table 4.

The first six curriculum subject definitions provide the basis for much of the data collection in later sections of the report. More than 80 per cent of the teachers gave us time-table answers using these terms, as set out in Table 4.

Table 4   *'How Does a Typical Pupil Spend the 27½ Hours of a Typical Week?'* Answers for Curriculum subjects

each line shows the percentage of teachers giving answers:	¼–1 hour per week	1¼–2 hours per week	2¼–3 hours per week	3¼–4 hours per week	4¼–5 hours per week	5¼–6 hours per week	6¼–7 hours per week	7¼–8 hours per week	8¼–9 hours per week	9¼–10 hours per week	no answer
Mathematics	1%	2%	10%	21%	33%	15%	4%	2%	0%	0%	12%
Language	1%	1%	2%	2%	8%	11%	19%	19%	14%	4%	19%
Thematic Studies	2%	9%	21%	17%	21%	7%	3%	2%	0%	0%	18%
Art and Craft	11%	39%	26%	4%	1%	0%	0%	0%	0%	0%	19%
Music	66%	22%	2%	0%	0%	0%	0%	0%	0%	0%	10%
Physical Education	3%	17%	37%	31%	4%	0%	0%	0%	0%	0%	8%
Integrated Studies	8%	7%	4%	2%	2%	0%	1%	1%	0%	0%	75%

N = 498 junior teachers. Horizontal rows total to 100%

Notes: 1   *'No answer' is difficult to interpret; in the case of 'Integrated Studies' it mostly means 'none', but for the other subjects it either means 'not disentangleable from Integrated Studies' or 'impossible to quantify'.*

      2   *As with most tables of this sort, there are dangers in the interpretation. The small amount of time apparently spent by some on mathematics and language may reflect formal lessons on these subjects while other work in these subjects is subsumed under 'Integrated Studies'.*

The third aspect of this question focuses on teaching methods. We identified four major teaching methods used by class teachers, viz:

Classwork	*Periods of time when the attention of the class is on the same work, either individually or collectively, e.g.* teacher giving instruction on mathematics to everybody; children doing sums individually from blackboard or workbooks; teacher reading story; all children painting; all children writing stories.
Groupwork in one subject	*Periods of time when only one subject is in progress but different groups are engaged in different aspects of it, either individually or collectively within the groups, e.g.* one group working individually on sums from 'The 4 Rules of Number', a second group working co-operatively in measuring the classroom, a third group engaged on work cards on shape, and a fourth group doing practical work with the teacher on capacity.
Groupwork in more than one subject	*Periods of time when different groups are engaged in different subjects, e.g.* one group is working at mathematics, a second group is writing stories, and a third group is doing some creative work.
Self-organized individual work on assignments	*Periods of time when children are engaged in individual studies across the curriculum which they have chosen to work at from a list of teacher-set assignments.*

One of the most pleasing outcomes of the Project is that this four-fold categorization of teaching methods works: most teachers were able to fit their pattern of activity into these categories. (A similar scheme was devised for describing the teaching methods of teachers working in teams, but since these teachers were only 6 per cent of the total this scheme is omitted from the report.) Table 5 gives the results of this part of the enquiry.

Because others may find the classification useful it is worth commenting on some features of it. The classification is about periods of time and about what all the children in the class are doing; the activity of the teacher is not specifically mentioned. 'Classwork' is defined as times when the class are all doing the same thing, whether actively or passively. Two forms of 'groupwork' are defined; different teachers are inclined to use this term with slightly different meanings and so it was important to tie definitions to the terms. It seems an important difference to distinguish between groupwork when only one subject is in progress and the other kind when several subjects are all in progress at once — this is sometimes called 'rotating groupwork'. Because we were able to collect our data in interviews it was possible to spend time explaining to each respondent what we meant by the terms.

Taking the mode for each item of tables 3, 4 and 5 it is possible (with minor adjustments) to construct an average time schedule for the junior classes in the survey. This is given in Table 6.

Which teaching methods are used most widely? The data from 454 junior teachers engaged in class teaching has been analyzed to find the numbers of teachers using the four major teaching methods for seven hours or more per week. It works out that 49 per cent of the teachers use only one of these major teaching methods for seven hours or more per week and 44 per cent use two of them. Only 3 per cent use such a variety of methods that no one features for as much as seven hours per week. The remaining 4 per cent of the teachers use 'other' methods predominately; these have not been identified. No use uses three of the major methods for seven or more hours each per week. The choice of seven hours as the dividing line is arbitrary (it is one quarter of the working

Table 5 'How Does a Typical Pupil Spend the 27½ Hours of a Typical Week?' Answers for the Different Kinds of Teaching Method

each line shows the percentages of teachers giving the answers	not used	¼-2 hours per week	2¼-4 hours per week	4¼-6 hours per week	6¼-8 hours per week	8¼-10 hours per week	10¼-12 hours per week	12¼-14 hours per week	14¼-16 hours per week	16+ hours per week	no answer
classwork	1%	4%	7%	15%	20%	16%	13%	6%	5%	6%	7%
groupwork in one subject	15%	14%	17%	17%	10%	8%	4%	3%	3%	2%	7%
groupwork in more than one subject	33%	10%	14%	12%	7%	7%	4%	2%	2%	2%	7%
self-organized individual work on assignments	37%	15%	14%	9%	5%	4%	4%	3%	1%	1%	7%
other	71%	11%	3%	1%	0%	0%	0%	0%	0%	0%	14%

N = 498 junior teachers. Horizontal rows total to 100%

Table 6   *'How Does a Typical Pupil Spend the 27½ Hours of a
Typical Week?' Average of the Answers for Juniors*

Mathematics	5	classwork	9
Language	7	groupwork in one subject	6
Thematic Studies	4		
Art and Craft	2	groupwork in more than one subject	4
Music	1		
Physical Education	3	self-organized individual work on assignments	3

(Mathematics through Physical Education braced together = 22)

assembly	2
administration	1
playtimes	2½
total	27½ hours per week

week and one third of the working week less administration,
assembly and playtimes); its justification is that it reveals the
relative popularities of different teaching methods. Table 6A
shows that classwork is the most widely practised method.

Table 6A   *'Which Teaching Methods Predominate?'
This Table gives the Percentages of Teachers Using Stated
Methods for Seven Hours or More per Week*

Classwork	24
Classwork + groupwork in one subject	17
Classwork + groupwork in several subjects	14
Groupwork in one subject	11
Groupwork in several subjects	8
Classwork + self-organized individual work	8
Self-organized individual work	6
Other methods	4
Variety of methods — none for 7 hours or more per week	3
Groupwork in one subject + groupwork in several subjects	2
Groupwork in one subject + self-organized individual work	2
Groupwork in several subjects + self-organized individual work	1

N = 454 junior teachers. Column totals 100%. Items in rank order.

We asked how the places were arranged for classwork; 58 per cent responded that the places were 'allocated by the teacher', 33 per cent said 'most or all of the children choose their own place'. (9 per cent either did not reply or used 'other' ways of arranging places).

In 36 per cent of the classes 'groupwork in more than one subject' entailed 'fixed groups', *i.e.* children always in the same grouping. We asked these teachers to indicate if *one* of a list of criteria for grouping was the main procedure used; if several or other criteria were in use, then 'other' was to be ticked. The responses are given in Table 7.

Table 7   *Criteria for Setting Up Groups of the 36% of Teachers who use Fixed Groups for Groupwork in more than One Subject*

reading attainment	10%
mathematics attainment	5%
random allocation by teacher	5%
free choice by children	3%
age	0%
separate sexes	0%
other (including several of the above)	13%
	36%

N = 180 junior teachers, ie 36% of the total. Items listed in rank order

For 56 per cent of the classes we were told about the way in which self-organized assignment work is programmed. Five systems were put forward on the interview schedule and teachers were asked to tick one of these, or 'other'. The results are in Table 8. (Table 5 shows that 37 per cent do not use self-organized assignment work; the remaining 7 per cent gave no reply).

Table 8   *Methods of Programming Self-organized Assignment Work as Reported by 56% of the Teachers*

daily list	—on chalkboard, etc	12%	
	—issued to each pupil on an individual sheet or card on a regular basis	1%	
	—'daily' list sub-total		13%
weekly list	—on chalkboard, etc	4%	
	—issued to each pupil on an individual sheet or card on a regular basis	7%	
	—'weekly' list sub-total		11%
assignments given to pupils on an individual basis when previous ones completed			19%
other			13%
			56%

N = 279 junior teachers, ie 56% of the total. Items listed in logical order

The report now concentrates on the different areas of the curriculum.

Mathematics

Under this heading was included any activity where the main aim is to develop mathematical concepts and skills: instruction, work cards, exercises, practical mathematics, mental arithmetic, table recitations, etc.

We asked 'In what ways do your pupils spend their time on your mathematics programme?' The replies are given on Table 9.

Table 9   *Ways in which Children Spend their Time on Mathematics*

each line shows the percentages of teachers giving the answers:	'nearly all or most of the time'	'some of the time'	'a little or none of the time'
individually working at class textbooks	30%	49%	21%
individually working at home-made cards or work sheets	10%	44%	46%
individually working from commercial work cards or kits	8%	25%	67%
in groups working orally with the teacher	5%	57%	38%
individually working from chalkboard or from wall posters	3%	35%	62%
as a class working orally with the teacher	2%	51%	47%

N = 498 junior teachers. Horizontal rows total to 100%
Items in rank order of first column

These replies show the variety of ways in which mathematics is taught. It is clear that 'individually working at class text books' is the most prevalent way of working, but nevertheless 7 per cent of the teachers interviewed never use this approach. (14 per cent 'a little of the time' and 7 per cent 'none of the time', combined total 21 per cent. In several places in the text of the report more detailed figures will be given than in the tables.)

Other instances of teaching approaches not used are: 'as a class working orally with the teacher', *i.e.* class lessons, 8 per cent of the teachers indicated that they never work this way; likewise 17 per cent do not use home-made cards or worksheets and 27 per cent do not have children working from chalkboard or posters on the walls.

We asked whether the syllabus in mathematics, meaning a

list of content and skills, was mainly the teacher's own choice and design, or whether it was one which had been drawn up for the school. Half of the teachers replied that they were using their own design and half that they were using a school syllabus.

Class textbooks in mathematics were used by 93 per cent of the teachers; we asked for details of books, commercial work cards and kits and Table 10 gives a list of items mentioned by ten or more teachers.

Table 10   *Mathematics Textbooks in Common Use*

title and author(s) or publisher		% of teachers mentioning
'Alpha/Beta'	Goddard and Grattidge	54%
'Mathematics for Schools'	Fletcher	28%
'Four Rules' series	Hesse	22%
'Making Sure of Mathematics'	Watson and Quin	14%
'Five/Ten a Day'	Griffiths	9%
'Towards Mathematics'	Sturgess and Glenn	9%
'More Practice in Mathematics'	Adams and Beaumont	7%
'Let's Discover Mathematics'	Marsh	5%
'Mathematics at Work'	Forgan	4%
'Next Number Please'	Scofield and Sims	4%
'Graded Arithmetic Practice'	Hesse	3%
'Mathematics Adventure'	Stanfield	3%
'Problems' series	Hesse	3%
'Basic Mathematics'	Griffiths	3%
'Metrication Mathematics'	Saunders	3%
'Practical Mathematics'	Simcox	2%
'Starting Points'	Sims	2%

N = 498 junior teachers. '2%' or more listed. Items in rank order

We asked if any teacher's source books, other than class textbooks, were used. Table 11 gives books cited by five or more teachers.

Table 11   *Teachers' Books on Mathematics in Common Use*

title and author(s) or publisher		% of teachers mentioning
'Mathematics for Schools, Teacher's Resource Book'	Fletcher	22%
'Nuffield Mathematics, Project Guides and Check-ups'	Nuffield Foundation	7%
'Mathematics in Primary Schools' Curr. Bull. 1	Schools Council	4%
'Teaching of Arithmetic in Primary Schools'	Downes and Paling	2%
'Guidelines in School Mathematics'	Manchester College of Education	2%
'Mathematics through Discovery'	Whitaker	1%
'Primary Mathematics'	Mathematical Association	1%

N = 498 junior teachers. '1%' or more listed. Items in rank order

The teachers were asked in what ways they had determined the level of mathematical attainment of their children at the beginning of the year. For 80 per cent of the classes the teachers had received record card, check list or written notes from the previous teacher. Also, 60 per cent of the teachers tested the children at the beginning of the school year. The most common kind of test is that devised by the individual teacher, as is shown by Table 12.

Table 12   *Attainment Tests in Mathematics in Common Use*

title	% of teachers mentioning
'test devised by teacher for her own class'	31%
'test devised within the school for several classes'	17%
'NFER tests'	12%
'Hesse's tests'	9%
'Yardsticks'	2%
'Nottingham Number Test' — Gilham	1%

N = 498 junior teachers. '1%' or more listed. Items in rank order

Language

Under this heading was included any activity where the teacher's main aim is to promote language skills, *i.e.* reading aloud, reading silently, writing, talking, listening, comprehension, spelling, grammar, punctuation, handwriting, creative writing, etc. No language other than English was being taught in these schools.

We asked each teacher whether she had any deliberate procedures for promoting spoken language other than every-day class discussion and conversation. This was an open-ended question without prompting. Of the 498 junior teachers, 32 per cent indicated that they used drama with this aim in mind, 13 per cent referred to their use of tape recorders so that children could listen to their own voices and learn through this, and 4 per cent reported that they organized group discussions in their classes. Other teachers gave a range of miscellaneous answers which amounted to variants of classroom discussion — debates, children reporting on project work, etc. But 32 per cent gave no answer to this question.

A question asking about the amount of time spent on different kinds of writing activities produced a rather complicated set of answers which is not easy to analyze. However certain points are clear. By and large, these teachers put equal emphasis on descriptive writing (*i.e.* reporting, recording, describing) and on creative writing (*i.e.* stories, poetry). Most of the creative writing is of stories, but half of the classes spend 'some of the time' in writing poetry. Few try to write plays. Few use personal diaries as a writing activity.

Handwriting skills are taught by virtually all of the teachers; only 2 per cent said they spend 'none of the time' on this. Spelling tests are given by 83 per cent; dictation is given by only 23 per cent and not often. Nearly everybody uses comprehension and vocabulary exercises; 14 per cent for 'most of the time' and 65 per cent for 'some of the time'.

Only 19 per cent of the teachers worked to a school syllabus or policy for written language work; the others were

Table 13   *English Language Class Textbooks etc in Common Use*

title and author(s) or publisher		% of teachers mentioning
'Sound Sense'	Tansley	32%
'Better English Series'	Ridout	14%
'SRA Reading Laboratories'	SRA	13%
'Effective English'	Mountain and Barnes	9%
'Primary English'	Sanders	8%
'Ladybird Comprehension cards'	Wills and Hepworth	7%
'All Around English'	Ridout	6%
'Oxford Junior Workbooks'	Carver	5%
'Using Good English'	Dalzell	5%
'English for Primary Schools'	Cleland and Borely	4%
'Reading Routes'	Leedham	4%
'Reading to Some Purpose'	Ridout and Flowerdew	4%
'Spelling'	Smith	4%
'Sounds and Words'	Southgate	4%
'Reading Workshop'	Conochie	3%
'Exploration English'	Gagg	3%
'Read, Write and Remember'	Milburn	3%
'Passwords'	Rose and Young	3%
'English for Today'	Ballance	2%
'Using our Language'	Darley	2%
'Into English'	Edwards and Mays	2%
'Comprehension and Study cards'	Gregory	2%
'Understanding through Interest'	Hoare	2%
'English Workbooks'	Ridout	2%
'Complete English'	Thorpe	2%
'Sounds for Reading'	O'Donnell	2%

N = 498 junior teachers. '2%' or more listed. Items in rank order.
Each title represents a graded series of books, etc.

individually responsible for devising their own.

We asked what class text books or commercial work cards were in use. Table 13 lists the items mentioned by ten or more teachers.

Only a few teachers indicated that they use particular teachers' books as sources of ideas for English language teaching. Items mentioned five times or more are listed in Table 14.

Table 14   *Teachers' Books on English Language in Common Use*

title and author(s)		% of teachers mentioning
'First Aid in English'	MacIver	6%
'Ideas'	Ramsbottom	6%
'Wordscapes/Thoughtshapes'	Maybury	3%
'Creative Writing for Juniors'	Maybury	3%
'An Approach to Creative Writing in the Primary School'	Lane and Kemp	1%
'Towards Creative Writing'	Lane and Kemp	1%
'Bandwagon/Bandstand'	Maybury	1%
'Creative Themes'	Pluckrose	1%
'SRA Manual'		1%
'Spelling' (several books)	Schonell	1%

N = 498 junior teachers. '1%' or more listed. Items in rank order

We asked whether each teacher's reading policy was 'mainly her own' or 'mainly the school's'; 45 per cent gave the first answer and 55 per cent the second.

In enquiring into silent reading, we asked 'Of the time in school devoted to silent reading activities by your class, how much is spent on different forms of reading?' Five alternatives were suggested in the question and the responses are shown in the following table.

We also enquired about reading aloud. In 64 per cent of the classes, all of the children are required to read aloud regularly either to the teacher or to another adult; in the other classes only particular children have to read aloud in this way. In 10 per cent of the classes, all of the children are re-

Table 15   *Ways in which Children Spend their Time on Silent Reading*

each line shows the percentages of teachers giving the answers:	'nearly all or most of the time'	'some of the time'	'a little or none of the time'
general reading scheme (a structured sequence)	46%	33%	21%
library books (pupil chosen)	25%	51%	24%
reference books	6%	58%	36%
work cards	5%	43%	52%
class textbooks	5%	39%	56%

N = 498 junior teachers. Horizontal rows total to 100%
Items in rank order of first column

quired to read aloud to the class from time to time, but in 31 per cent of the classes none of the children do this.

We asked whether teachers had tested their children in terms of reading ability at the beginning of the school year; 48 per cent had. The tests used are listed in Table 16. Also, 82 per cent of the teachers had received from the class's previous teacher a record card, check list or written notes on the reading progress of every individual child. Other teachers test their children at other times of the year, for only 14 per cent of the teachers used no reading tests.

Table 16   *Reading Tests in Common Use*

	% of teachers mentioning
Burt	52%
Daniels and Diack	30%
Schonell	24%
Young	6%
NFER	4%
Holburn	2%
Neale	2%
Southgate	1%

N = 498 junior teachers. '1%' or more listed. Items in rank order.

Each teacher was asked if she read regularly to her class and if so what was the current book. From 88 per cent of the teachers such information was obtained. Table 17 contains a list of those books which were being read at the time of interview by five or more teachers. A full list is given in Appendix 1.

Table 17   *Most Popular Stories Read Aloud to Classes*

title and author		% of teachers reading the book at the time of the interview
'The Lion, The Witch and the Wardrobe'	Lewis	4%
'James and the Giant Peach'	Dahl	3%
'Stig of the Dump'	King	3%
'Charlie and the Chocolate Factory'	Dahl	2%
'Charlie and the Great Glass Elevator'	Dahl	2%
'Fantastic Mr Fox'	Dahl	2%
'The Silver Sword'	Serraillier	2%
'The Weirdstone of Brisingamen'	Garner	1%
'The Iron Man'	Hughes	1%
'A Hundred and One Dalmatians'	Smith	1%
'The Hobbit'	Tolkien	1%

N = 498 junior teachers. '1%' or more listed. Items in rank order

Thematic Studies

'Thematic studies' was a term introduced to embrace study of any subjects, topics or projects on scientific, geographic, environmental, historical or Biblical themes, carried out individually, in groups, or as a class, where the teacher's main aim is to provide experience of the subject matter and, or, to develop the skills of enquiry.

At each interview the research officer explained that we were using this unfamiliar expression in order to bring together the various curriculum activities listed above; had the term 'topic' or 'subjects' been used, it might have meant that some curriculum activities would have escaped notice. Of the 498 junior teachers interviewed, only 2 per cent were unable to respond to the questions about 'thematic studies'.

Table 18   *The Most Popular 'Themes' or Topics*

title	% of teachers mentioning	title	% of teachers mentioning
'Animals'	18%	'Weather'	4%
'Other countries'	14%	'Farms'	4%
'Local environment'	13%	'Holidays'	4%
'Autumn'	12%	'London'	4%
'Christmas'	10%	'Birds'	3%
'Queen's Jubilee'	9%	'Canals and rivers'	3%
'Famous people'	7%	'Health themes'	3%
'Foods'	7%	'Polar regions'	3%
'Police'	7%	'Post office'	3%
'The body (and parts)'	6%	'Railways'	3%
'Homes and houses'	6%	'Tudor England'	3%
'Biblical themes'	6%	'Energy (coal, oil, etc)'	3%
'Nottingham'	6%	'Spring'	3%
'Fifth of November'	6%	'Stone age man'	3%
'Flight (and aircraft)'	6%	'Clothing and costume'	3%
'Transport'	6%	'North American Indians'	3%
'Time'	5%	'Romans'	3%
'Goose Fair'	5%	'Communications'	3%
'Winter'	5%	'Explorers'	3%
'People who help us'	5%	'British Isles'	3%
'Ourselves'	5%	'Conservation/pollution'	2%
'Trees'	5%	'Newspapers'	2%
'Fire'	4%	'Story themes'	2%
'Hallowe'en'	4%	'The Earth'	2%
'Nature study'	4%	'Holes'	2%
'Colours'	4%	'Maps'	2%
'Seas'	4%	'Television'	2%
'Solar system/universe'	4%	'The senses'	2%

N = 498 junior teachers. '2%' or more listed. Items in rank order.
Note: Some of the titles listed in the Appendix have been collated here. Thus 'Animals' includes 'Pets', 'Mammals', 'Cats', 'Snakes', etc.

Analysis of the weekly timetables shows that 68 per cent of the teachers provide a curriculum activity called 'topic'; very few use the term 'project' (7 per cent). 'History' and 'geography' feature in the weekly timetables of 7 per cent and 6 per cent respectively of the teachers; 'science' in the timetables of 12 per cent. These three subjects are not mentioned in the timetables of 81 per cent.

We asked for the titles of themes already studied during the current year, in progress, or planned, and this resulted in a list of 567 items which reads like the index to an encyclopaedia! Table 18 gives the themes mentioned by 10 or more teachers; the full list is set out in Appendix 2.

Few schools or teachers seem to have an overall plan for thematic studies. Only 8 per cent of the teachers reported that they were working to a school scheme. Of the teachers interviewed during term one (N = 266) of the school year (autumn term) only 30 per cent were able to tell us the titles of the themes which they planned to develop during the rest of the school year.

Analysis of the replies obtained in term two (winter/spring term) showed how many themes each teacher had used in term one. These are set out in Table 19.

Table 19   *Numbers of Themes Developed in One Term by Different Teachers*

number of 'themes' developed during the autumn term	0	1	2	3	4	5	6	7 plus
percentage of teachers using each number of 'themes'	2%	22%	34%	18%	13%	6%	3%	2%

N = 234 junior teachers. Row totals 100%

A similar picture is presented in Table 20 which gives answers to the question 'Of the time devoted to "thematic studies", how much is spent on activities lasting no more than a day, a week, a half term, etc.'

Table 20   *Duration of 'Thematic Studies'*

each line shows the percentages of teachers giving the answers:	'nearly all or most of the time'	'some of the time'	'a little or none of the time'
activities lasting no more than a half-term	55%	28%	15%
activities lasting more than a half-term	15%	22%	61%
activities lasting no more than a week	6%	34%	58%
activities lasting no more than a day	2%	24%	72%

N = 498 junior teachers. Horizontal rows total 98%; a further 2% do no 'thematic studies'. Items in rank order of first column.

A question which sought to identify whether class, group or individual activities predominate and whether activities are chosen by teacher or by children, gave answers which are difficult to interpret. It seems however that 'thematic studies' are commonly tackled as class or group activities — the former being more common, and individually planned 'thematic studies' are rare. Teachers and children appear to be equally involved in choice of activity, but whether this means that the teacher chooses the overall theme and the children then decide on what aspect of it they will work on is not clear.

We asked to what extent 'thematic studies' helps children to learn enquiry skills, such as the use of an index, use of source books, library classification of books, etc. Very few teachers said 'not at all' (3 per cent); 49 per cent said 'to some extent' and 46 per cent said 'to a considerable extent'. Structured exercises in enquiry skills are used by 30 per cent of the teachers.

Most teachers organize visits linked to 'thematic studies'; only 1 in 12 doesn't. Table 21 shows the number of half days in the school year when teachers expect to be on visits connected with 'thematic studies'.

Table 21   *Number of Visits Linked to 'Thematic Studies' Made in
             One Year*

number of half days estimated to be spent on visits	0	1-2	3-4	5-6	7 plus
percentage of teachers in each set	8%	32%	29%	14%	15%

N = 498 junior teachers. Percentages total 98%; 2% do no 'thematic studies

Art and Craft

This heading was taken to include all art and craft activities where the main aims are to promote non-verbal imagination and expression and, or, manual skills which facilitate creative expression.

Perhaps the most interesting aspect of art and craft teaching to enquire into would be the extent to which teachers structure the experience of children. We spent some time trying to devise questions which would unambiguously investigate this topic, but failed to find an appropriate form of words and eventually, with regret, shelved the matter. Instead we asked about activities and source books.

Table 22 gives the rank order of time spent on nine specified art and craft activities by the 498 teachers overall; painting is the most popular activity in terms of time spent.

We asked what other art and craft activities were carried out. Answers included: basket work, batique, enamelling,

Table 22   *Art and Craft Activities: Rank Order of Time Spent on
             Nine Items*

1	painting
2	drawing
3	claywork
4	collage
5	woodwork
6	needlework
7	cooking
8	modelmaking
9	fabric dyeing

*N = 498 junior teachers. Note: 'other' scored 10 in the rank order;
examples of other activities are listed above.*

knitting, lino cut work, marbling, montage, nail and thread work, paper sculpture, papier mache, photography, plaster cast work, printing, rubbings, scissor work, straw craft, tinfoil sculpture, and weaving.

Only 3 per cent of the teachers said that they were working mainly to a school syllabus in art and craft.

We asked about source books and commercial work cards, etc. Table 23 gives the few items mentioned ten times or more.

Table 23   *Art and Craft Books in Common Use*

title and author or publisher		% of teachers mentioning
'Art and Crafts in the Primary School'	Pluckrose	5%
'Starting Points'	Pluckrose	3%
'Colour Craft Series'	MacDonald	2%

N = 498 junior teachers. '2%' or more listed. Items in rank order

Music

This heading was taken to include singing, making music and listening to music. The extent to which these three activities occur is shown in Table 24.

Table 24   *Ways in Which Children Spend Their Time on Music*

each line shows the percentages of teachers giving the answers:	'nearly all or most of the time'	'some of the time'	'a little or none of the time'
singing	70%	19%	6%
making music	5%	31%	59%
listening to music	1%	29%	65%

N = 498 junior teachers. Horizontal rows total 95%; 5% gave no reply. Items in rank order of first column.

Music teaching entails considerable interchange between teachers and classes. We asked if the music activities were carried out by a colleague; 39 per cent of the teachers indicated that this was the case for their classes for singing, 30 per cent for 'making music' and 16 per cent for 'listening to music'.

Only 15 per cent of the teachers reported that they were working to a school syllabus in music.

Of the teachers making music with their classes, it seems that all engage in rhythmic percussion, just under half in tuned or melodic percussion, and just under half use recorders. Of all 498 teachers interviewed, 20 per cent play the recorder in school, 15 per cent play the piano and 13 per cent play the guitar. Also a further 5 per cent play other instruments in school — but we didn't ascertain what these are.

We asked for the name of any music and singing books used by class or teacher; Table 25 lists the replies given by 5 or more teachers.

Table 25   *Music and Singing Books Used by Class or Teacher*

title and author(s) or publisher		% of teachers mentioning
'Apusskidu'	Harrop (editor)	17%
'Singing Together'	BBC	17%
'Time and Tune' pamphlets	BBC	9%
'Oxford Junior Song Book'	Fiske and Dobbs	2%
'Music Time' pamphlets	BBC	2%
'Oxford School Music Book'	Fiske and Dobbs	2%
'Okki Tokki Unga'	Harrop (editor)	2%
'Someone's Singing Lord'	Black	2%
'Music Makers'	BBC	1%
'Carol Gaily Carol'	Harrop (editor)	1%

N = 498 junior teachers. '1%' or more listed. Items in rank order.

The teachers were asked whether they used ideas from any well-known method of teaching music as the basis of their work. Few said 'Yes'; of the 498 teachers, 7 per cent cited

Orff, 2 per cent Kodaly, and 2 per cent Dankworth and Baseter.

Where teachers played recorded music to their pupils we asked for the titles of three recent pieces. Items mentioned by five or more teachers are listed in Table 26. Classical music predominates.

Table 26   *Popular Music for Class Listening*

title and composer		% of teachers mentioning
Classical		
'The Planets' Suite'	Holst	8%
'Peter and the Wolf'	Prokofiev	8%
'Carnival of the Animals'	Saint-Saens	6%
'The Sorcerer's Apprentice'	Dukas	5%
'Peer Gynt Suite'	Grieg	4%
'Danse Macabre'	Saint-Saens	4%
'Scheherezade'	Rimsky-Korsakov	2%
'William Tell Overture'	Rossini	2%
'1812 Overture'	Tchaikovsky	2%
'Fingal's Cave'	Mendelssohn	1%
'Night on a Bare Mountain'	Mussorgsky	1%
'Nutcracker Suite'	Tchaikovsky	1%
'Coppelia'	Delibes	1%
'The Firebird'	Stravinsky	1%
'Pictures from an Exhibition'	Mussorgsky	1%
'Royal Fireworks Music'	Handel	1%
Film, Pop, Folk Music, etc.		
'Joseph and the Amazing Technicolour Dreamcoat'		2%
'Tubular Bells'	Oldfield	2%
'Oliver'		1%
'Spinners'		1%
'Albatross'	Fleetwood Mac	1%
'Young Person's Guide to the Orchestra'	Britten	1%

N = 498 junior teachers. '1%' or more listed. Items in rank order

Physical Education

It may seem unnecessary to define what is meant by

'physical education', but, having defined the other areas of the curriculum, it seemed necessary to do the same in this case. It was taken to include all activities such as apparatus work, movement, out-of-doors activities, swimming and games where the main aim is to promote the physical co-ordination of the body, body awareness and the acquisition of social and physical skills.

We asked 'Of the time which your class spends on physical education in school time, how much time is devoted to the following seven activities?' The seven items, and the collated replies, are given in Table 27.

Table 27　　*Ways in which Children Spend their Time in Physical Education*

each line shows the percentages of teachers giving the answers:	'most of the time'	'some of the time'	'a little or none of the time'
floorwork	11%	72%	15%
games skills	7%	72%	19%
large apparatus	6%	76%	16%
major team games	5%	49%	44%
swimming	4%	71%	23%
minor team games	2%	53%	43%
music and movement/dance	2%	44%	52%

N = 498 junior teachers. Horizontal rows total 98%; 2% gave no reply. Items in rank order of first column.

Only 12 per cent of the teachers worked to a school syllabus in physical education.

Table 28 gives the replies to the request for details of source books used by teachers in physical education. Items mentioned by 5 or more teachers are listed.

We asked about children with physical problems. 'Other than any children recognized as "physically handicapped", are there children in your class with poor muscular co-ordination, poor posture, or flat feet?' We did not enquire as to how many such children there were, but simply whether there were any. That there was at least one child in the class

Table 28   *Teachers' Books on Physical Education in Common Use*

title and author(s) or publisher		% of teachers mentioning
'A Physical Education Programme for Juniors'	Mitchell*	34%
'Gymnastics'	Buckland	5%
'Swimming'	ASA	4%
'Educational Gymnastics'	ILEA	4%
'PE in the Primary School'	Bilbrough and Jones	3%
'PE is Fun'	Brown*	2%
'Games and Sports'	Wise	2%
'BAGA Awards'	BAGA	1%
'Moving and Growing'	HMSO	1%
'Planning the Programme'	HMSO	1%
'Creative Dance in the Primary School'	Russell	1%

N = 498 junior teachers. '1%' or more listed. Items in rank order.
* Booklets by Notts LEA advisers.

with poor muscular co-ordination, was reported by 38 per cent of the teachers; 7 per cent reported that there was at least one child with poor posture; 10 per cent reported on the presence of flat feet. ('Poor muscular co-ordination' was defined in the question as meaning 'very clumsy, physically awkward or accident prone'; 'poor posture' was taken to mean 'abnormal curvature of the spine when sitting').

We asked for an estimate of the number of half-days during the school year when the class would be out of school 'mainly for physical education objectives'. In most cases this meant swimming. While 27 per cent of the teachers answered 'none', 62 per cent indicated that their classes would be out on ten or more occasions.

The report now focuses on some general matters.

Marking

We asked three questions about marking, which are set out, with the answers given, in tables 29, 30 and 31. We gave a rather broad meaning to the word mark: 'any form of response to your pupils' written work — such as spoken comment, written comment, numerical mark, etc.'

Table 29   *'How Much of your Pupils' Writing and Mathematics do you Mark?'*

percentages of teachers giving the answers:	'all or nearly all'	'most'	'some'
	91%	7%	0%

N = 498 junior teachers. Row totals 98%; no answer given by 2%

Table 30   *'Of the Writing and Mathematics that you Mark, can you Estimate how much is Marked in the Presence of, or in the Absence of, the Pupil?'*

percentages of teachers giving the answers'	'all or most'	'some'	'a little or none'
'marked in the pupil's presence'	55%	36%	7%
'marked in the pupil's absence but discussed individually with him when returned'	18%	50%	30%
'marked in the pupil's absence and without individual discussion on return'	3%	22%	73%

N = 498 junior teachers. Horizontal rows total 98%; no answer given by 2%. Items in rank order of first column.

Table 31   *'Which of These Forms of Response to Individual Children do you Use, and how Often?'*

percentages of teachers giving the answers:	'frequently'	'sometimes'	'rarely or never'
'tick'	54%	33%	11%
'extended spoken comment' *eg* discussion of work '	45%	46%	7%
'brief spoken comment' *eg* 'well done'	43%	50%	5%
'brief written comment' ` *eg* 'neat'	33%	54%	11%
'extended written comment' *eg* commentary on work'	14%	37%	47%
'star'	11%	21%	66%
'housepoint'	10%	11%	77%
'numerical mark, *eg* '5/10'	2%	11%	85%
'grade *eg* 'C'	1%	2%	95%

N = 498 junior teachers. Horizontal rows total 98%; no answer given by 2%. Items in rank order of first column.

These tables show that nearly every teacher tries to mark more or less all of her pupils' work and that marking in the pupils' presence is for many teachers important. While nearly everybody uses the tick to convey approval it is clear from Table 31 that comments are more important than numerical marks or grades — these being quite rare.

Record Keeping and Destiny of Completed Work

We asked about records of the work done by the class or by groups within the class, and about notes of individual children's difficulties and successes. The replies are shown in Table 32.

We asked what happens to children's work when it is completed and asked teachers to reply in terms of seven possibilities. The replies are shown in tables 33 and 34.

Table 32 *Records. 'In which Subjects do you keep Written Records of the Work Done by the Class or by Groups within the Class?' 'Do you keep Notes of Individual Children's Difficulties and Successes?'*

The tables show the percentages of teachers saying 'Yes, I keep this kind of record'

	Notes of work done	Notes of individual's difficulties and successes
Mathematics	84%	73%
Reading	82%	76%
Written Language	72%	63%
Thematic Studies	65%	37%
Art and Craft	36%	28%
Physical Education	32%	34%
Spoken Language	27%	45%
Music	20%	18%
Integrated Studies *	16%	10%

*N = 498 junior teachers. 98% of the teachers responded. Items in rank order of first column. * Less than 25% of teachers take 'Integrated Studies'.*

Table 34 *'What Happens to Children's Art and Craft Work when it is Completed?'*

each line shows the percentages of	'always or frequently'	'sometimes'	'rarely or never'
'displayed on wall'	81%*	16%	0%
'taken home'	31%	52%	14%
'stored in folder/tray until end of term'	19%	31%	47%
'stored in folder/tray until end of school year'	15%	24%	58%
'thrown away during term'	10%	51%	36%
'kept for record purposes'	5%	19%	73%
'thrown away immediately'	1%	19%	77%

*N = 498 junior teachers. Horizontal rows total to 97%; 3% gave no answers. Items in rank order of first column. * 74% were 'frequently'.*

Table 33   *'What happens to Children's Written Work when it is Completed?'*

each lines shows the percentages of teachers giving the answers:	'always or frequently'	'sometimes'	'rarely or never'
'stored in folder/tray until end of school year'	58%	21%	18%
'displayed on wall'	57%*	39%	1%
'stored in folder/tray until end of term'	50%	21%	26%
'kept for record purposes'	27%	39%	31%
'thrown away during term'	25%	21%	51%
'taken home'	15%	46%	36%
'thrown away immediately'	0%	2%	95%

*N = 498 junior teachers. Horizontal rows total to 97%; 3% gave no answers. Items in rank order of first column.   * 54% were 'frequently'*

Table 35   *'What Criteria do you Apply when Choosing Work for Class Wall Display?'*

each line shows the percentages of teachers giving the answers:	'always or frequently'	'sometimes'	'rarely or never'
'motivation of individual child'	52%	38%	7%
'cross-section of all work'	48%	35%	14%
'best work from the class'	31%	45%	21%

N = 498 junior teachers. Horizontal rows total to 97%; 3% gave no answers. Items in rank order of first column.

We also asked what criteria teachers used when choosing work for display on the classroom wall. How often is it motivation of the individual child, and is a cross-section of all work displayed or the best work from the class? The replies are in table 35.

Children with Special Needs

We asked each teacher whether there were children (one or more) in her class whom she considered to be seriously lacking in mathematics, spoken language, written language or reading. The definition of 'seriously lacking' was left to the individual teacher's judgment. Only 2 per cent of the 498 teachers declined to reply. Answers of 'Yes' were given as follows: reading 83 per cent, written language 79 per cent, mathematics 71 per cent, spoken language 56 per cent. As an **open-ended question** (*i.e.* **without any prompting of possible answers**) we enquired into what special provision, if any, was made for such children. It is always difficult to collate open-ended answers, but roughly 54 per cent of the teachers indicated that they enlist the remedial help of another teacher (head, deputy, fellow class teacher or, in some large schools, a specifically remedial teacher) and 30 per cent said that they organize individual work themselves for the children in special need. The services of speech therapists were cited by 5 per cent of the teachers.

Another question looked at the opposite end of the ability spectrum and asked 'Are there any very able children in your class who really need special work programmes in order to make the best use of their time in school?' Answers of 'Yes' were given by 42 per cent of the teachers and they indicated that they endeavour to provide individual forms of work for these children.

A third question about children with special needs enquired about disruptive children. 'Are there any children in your class who are particularly disruptive in that they regularly interfere with the learning of other children?' 'Yes' was the reply of 43 per cent of the teachers. In reply to the open-ended question about special provision, five major answers were given: 'isolate the disruptive child' was the answer of 15 per cent of the teachers, 'provide extra attention' said 10 per cent, 'move child to position where teacher can give increased supervision' said 5 per cent, 'punish or withdraw privileges' said another 5 per cent and 'refer to a child psychologist' said another 5 per cent.

(In each case the percentages given above are of N = 498 junior teachers).

Assembly

We asked each teacher what she did when her class attended assembly and offered four alternatives, recognizing that people might say 'Yes' to as many as were appropriate. We also asked how many times in a term the teacher was responsible for assembly, including times when her class was providing it. The answers are in tables 36 and 37.

Table 36   *'What do you do when your Class is at Assembly?'*

	% of teachers mentioning
'attend assembly'	87%
'prepare teaching, mark, make displays, etc'	52%
'meet with other staff'	32%
'work with a small group of remedial children'	16%

N = 498 junior teachers, but 3% gave no reply. Items in rank order.

Table 37   *'How Often per Term are you Responsible for an Assembly (Including when your Class is Providing it)?'*

number of assemblies taken per term	none	1	2	3	4	5-9	10 plus
percentage of teachers in each set	13%	17%	19%	14%	9%	8%	17%

N = 498 junior teachers, but 3% gave no reply.

Radio and Television Programmes used in School

We enquired into the television and radio broadcasts used in school. Only 13 per cent of the teachers make no regular use of broadcasts; on average each teacher uses 2½ broadcasts, but such data is better expressed as a frequency distribution, as in table 38.

Table 38   *'How many Television or Radio Programmes Does your Class Watch or Listen to Regularly?'*

percentage of teachers replying	'no programmes'	'one programme'	'two programmes'	'three programmes'	'four programmes'	'five or more programmes'
Radio	43%	31%	17%	5%	2%	1%
Television	21%	30%	33%	11%	3%	2%
Radio and Television	13%	17%	26%	18%	15%	10%

N = 498 junior teachers. Horizontal rows total 99%; 1% gave no answer.

Of the total number of broadcasts received by the classes in the survey, 40 per cent were radio and 60 per cent television; 73 per cent were 'off-air' and 27 per cent recorded and played back in school. (Unfortunately we failed to find out how many schools used video recording equipment). Radio Nottingham broadcasts for schools were used by 9 per cent of the teachers.

We asked whether programmes were 'central or peripheral to teaching'. The teachers' replies indicated that they felt that 40 per cent of the broadcasts were central to their work. We also asked whether the teachers used any printed material linked to the programmes: the answer was 'yes' for 68 per cent of the broadcasts.

Table 39 gives an analysis of the programmes used by 3 per cent and more of the teachers.

Table 39   *Popular Radio and Television Broadcasts for Schools*

Programme title	Source	% of teachers using it
'Singing Together'	BBC radio	14%
'Merry Go Round'	BBC TV	13%
'Time and Tune'	BBC radio	13%
'Movement, Music and Drama'	BBC radio	12%
'Finding Out'	ITV	11%
'Look and Read'	BBC TV	10%
'Picture Box'	ITV	10%
'Science All Around Us'	BBC TV	8%
'Stop, Look and Listen'	ITV	8%
'Over to You'	ITV	8%
'How We Used to Live'	ITV	8%
'Stories and Rhymes'	BBC radio	7%
'Watch'	BBC TV	7%
'Living Language'	BBC radio	6%
'Words and Pictures'	BBC TV	6%
'Out of the Past'	BBC TV	6%
'A Service for Schools'	BBC radio	5%
'Maths Workshop'	BBC TV	5%
'Music Time'	BBC TV	5%
'Near and Far'	BBC TV	5%
'Figure it Out'	ITV	5%
'Nature'	BBC radio	5%
'Meeting our Needs'	ITV	4%
'Spring Board'	BBC radio	4%
'Good Health'	ITV	3%
'Nottingham Ghosts'	Radio Nottingham	3%
'Look Around'	ITV	3%
'History: Long Ago'	BBC radio	3%
'Electric Company'	BBC TV	3%

N = 498 junior teachers. 1% gave no answer to this question. '3%' or more listed. Items in rank order.

Visits and Visitors

At least 90 per cent of the teachers organize visits for their classes during school time in the school year. It is not easy to analyze the data that our questions brought but table 40 gives an indication of the kinds of places visited.

Table 40   *Places Visited by Teachers with Children During Previous Year*

	% of times mentioned
Places in Nottinghamshire (in the vicinity of the school or further afield)	25%
Museums	15%
Parks, nature reserves, woodland, etc	15%
Places outside Nottinghamshire and Derbyshire (not listed elsewhere, usually towns)	14%
Cinemas, theatres, concerts	10%
Places in Derbyshire	7%
Zoos	5%
Stately homes and castles (excluding museums)	4%
Exhibitions	3%
Churches and cathedrals	2%

*N = circa 1400 visits. Column totals 100%. Items in rank order.
Note that there are difficulties in categorising some items.*

We enquired about any 'visitors who have talked to or worked with your class during the past twelve months either in classroom or assembly'. One quarter of the classes had had no such visitors during the past year; details of numbers of visitors are given in Table 41.

Table 41   *Number of Visitors Received during Past Year who have Talked to or Worked with the Class either in Classroom or Assembly*

number of visitors	none	1	2	3	4	5-9	10 plus
percentage of teachers in each set	27%	23%	17%	13%	7%	8%	5%

Table 42 shows some of the categories of visitors, the police being the most common. Over a third of the visitors come in a miscellaneous category including people such as the Lord Mayor of Nottingham, a Grenadier guardsman, a mushroom expert, a lollipop lady, a missionary, a lion club owner and a chimney sweep. One or two replies included 'headteacher'; it wasn't clear whether this was the school's own head or not!

Table 42   *Category List of Visitors*

	% of teachers mentioning
Police	37%
Clergy	18%
Age concern etc	9%
Parents (variety of topics)	8%
Road Safety Officers (other than police)	6%
Children's welfare societies	6%
Musicians	6%
Theatre groups etc	5%
Animal welfare societies	3%
Fire Brigade	2%

N = 498 junior teachers of whom 73% organize visitors.
Items in rank order.

PART III INFANT TEACHERS

Introduction

In total 281 infant teachers were interviewed. These were all teachers with registration groups; 'floating' teachers and part-time teachers were not interviewed. Also probationary teachers were excluded. Neither were nursery teachers interviewed. Of these 281 teachers, 79 per cent taught in Nottingham, 11 per cent in Gedling and 10 per cent in Newark. The following table shows the extent to which we sampled all of the teachers in each area.

Table 43   *Percentages of Infant Teachers in each Area Interviewed*

	Nottingham	Gedling	Newark	Nottingham, Gedling and Newark combined
percentage of all the infant teachers in the area who were interviewed	43%	23%	17%	35%

Throughout the report 'infant' means children aged 5 to 7 and 'primary' means children aged 5 to 11. (Children approaching their 5th birthday and in infant schools have been included as 5 year olds). In types of school, 55 per cent of the infant teachers interviewed were in infant schools and 45 per cent in primary schools.

In terms of buildings, 70 per cent of the teachers worked in classrooms, 7 per cent in open plan areas, and 23 per cent in 'semi-open spaces'; the latter term implying a classroom area plus an adjacent space which is usually shared with other classes.

The three age groups of infant children were equally represented in the interviews. Teachers were asked, 'What is the age range of most of the children taught by you most of the time; 1st year infant, 2nd year infant, 3rd year infant, 1st year junior?' They could tick as many of these as seemed appropriate. The responses show that 57 per cent were teaching all three infant age groups together (vertical grouping), 28 per cent were teaching two age groups together (transitional grouping), and the remaining 15 per cent were teaching one age group alone (age grouping). Only 2 per cent of the teachers ticked '1st year junior', thus indicating that they had a grouping of both infants and juniors in significant numbers.

Nearly everybody worked as a class teacher: 96 per cent. The rest consisted of 2 per cent working in teams of three and 2 per cent who worked partly with one class but also partly with other classes and felt that they were neither 'class' nor 'team' teachers.

We asked how many children each teacher had on her register. (In a team situation the total number of children was to be divided by the number of teachers). Table 44 gives the findings.

Table 44   *Sizes of Classes*

number of children in the class	up to 14	15-19	20-24	25-29	30-34	35-39	40+
percentage of teachers working with each size of class	1%	5%	23%	39%	26%	5%	1%

N = 281 infant teachers. The row totals 100%. Interviews November 1976 — March 1977.

The next section of the report deals with timetables, with the use of time for different parts of the curriculum, and with some of the ways in which teaching is organized.

Timetables and the Use of Time

We asked 'How does a typical pupil spend the 25 hours of a typical week?' Seven categories for the answer were suggested, with definitions as follows.

'Administration' Registration, dinner money, milk, handwashing, tidying up, etc. Research officers stressed that this was to be seen as an integral part of the educational programme.

'Class Talk' Discussion, news, story — led by the teacher. This implies that all of the class are participating together in a talking and listening activity.

'Activity Time' Times when individual work, group work or class work take place on reading, writing, number, topic, creative art work, classroom play activities, etc.

Play Time Play time as a fixed event when the children go outside the classroom.

Assembly Times when several classes, etc. meet together.

Physical Education Physical education with or without apparatus; music and movement, etc.

Other This was left in order to cover items overlooked. In the event some teachers used this heading to cover music and singing, others used it for television sessions.

Table 45   *'How Does a Typical Pupil Spend the 25 Hours of a Typical Week?' Answers for 'Activity Time'*

percentage of teachers giving answers:	under 6 hours per week	6¼-8 hours per week	8¼-10 hours per week	10¼-12 hours per week	12¼-14 hours per week	14¼-16 hours per week	16¼-18 hours per week	18 plus hours per week
'activity time'	11%	2%	8%	25%	35%	22%	5%	1%

N = 281 infant teachers. Row totals to 99%; 1% gave no answer.

Table 46   *'How Does a Typical Pupil Spend the 25 Hours of a Typical Week?' Answers for Items other than 'Activity Time'*

each line shows the percentage of teachers giving the answers:	0 hours per week	¼-1 hours per week	1¼-2 hours per week	2¼-3 hours per week	3¼-4 hours per week	4¼-5 hours per week	5¼-6 hours per week	over 6 hours per week
'administration'	1%	16%	34%	33%	9%	4%	1%	1%
'class talk'	1%	3%	8%	25%	31%	25%	4%	2%
play time	9%	4%	14%	71%*	1%	0%	0%	0%
assembly	0%	12%	58%	29%	0%	0%	0%	0%
physical education	1%	24%	53%	19%	2%	0%	0%	0%
other	32%	39%	18%	5%	2%	0%	1%	2%

N = 281 infant teachers. Row totals to 99%; 1% gave no answer. *68% replied 2½ hours per week.

Although some teachers found it not easy to analyze their time in these terms, with the assistance of the research officers all but 1 per cent gave replies in the format described. The answers are set out in Tables 45 and 46.

Taking the mode for each item in Tables 43 and 44 it is possible (with minor adjustments) to construct an average time schedule for the infant classes in the survey. This is given in Table 47.

Table 47   *'How Does a Typical Pupil Spend the 25 hours of a Typical Week?' Average of the Answers for Infants.*

'activity time'	13	hours
'class talk'	3½	hours
play time	2½	hours
'administration'	2	hours
assembly	2	hours
physical education	1½	hours
other	½	hour
	25	hours per week

In the above tables 'play time' was defined as a fixed event when the children go outside the classroom. We asked for further details and presented each respondent with five alternatives, one of which was to be ticked. The replies are given in Table 48 and show that three quarters of the classes surveyed work to a system in which there is a clear cut play time each morning and each afternoon.

Table 48   *'Do You Have a Fixed Play Time'*

	% of teachers indicating 'Yes'
fixed time every morning and afternoon	76%
fixed time every afternoon only	9%
no fixed times	7%
fixed time every morning only	3%
fixed times some days, not others	1%

N = 281 infant teachers. Row totals to 96%; no answer from 4%. Items in rank order.

Three patterns of organization of 'activity time' are used in Nottinghamshire infant schools, either singly or in combination. Instead of asking whether teachers worked 'formally' or used 'the integrated day', we asked a more sophisticated question in which these three patterns were defined.

'What organizational pattern do you use at present for 'activity time'?

Pattern 1   This is where the *whole class* starts to do 'mathematics' at the same time (all doing the same, or working in groups, or working individually), and likewise starts to do 'writing' at another time and so on.

Pattern 2   This is where the class is divided into *groups with fixed membership* and one group starts work with 'mathematics', while another starts with 'writing' and another starts with 'art', for example.

Pattern 3   This is where *individual decisions* are made at each activity time for each child (either by him or by the teacher) as to whether he does 'mathematics' or 'writing' or 'art' etc.

If you use more than one pattern, please indicate.'

The answers given to this question are in Table 49. It is particularly pleasing that teachers found themselves able to answer this question since the format of the three patterns is not one that would have been familiar to many of them. As with other parts of the enquiry, this success is partly due to the question being put orally by a research officer who could explain the terms in use.

As an open-ended question we asked the teachers for a simple description of their organizational pattern. It is not possible to collate these descriptions, but the following

Table 49   *'What Organizational Pattern do you Use at Present for 'Activity Time'?'*

		% of teachers working to each pattern
Pattern 1	(whole class working at same activity — together, in groups or individually)	4%
Patterns 1 and 2		3%
Pattern 2	(class divided into fixed groups which are working at different activities)	15%
Patterns 2 and 3		33%
Pattern 3	(individual decisions about activities — made by teacher or by child)	42%

N = 281 infant teachers. Column totals 97%. No reply from 3%. Items in logical order.

extracts from replies give an indication of the variety of ways in which infant classes are organized.

Teacher A   Pattern 1; 3rd year class

'After registration and administration there is physical education every day. Then comes maths followed by language (reading, writing and talking). This morning pattern continues into the afternoon if work is unfinished. The afternoon is mainly creative work and music, with the last half hour spent on a story or poetry appreciation'.

Teacher B   Pattern 1; vertically grouped class

'Number in the morning before play time and reading activities and writing after. Art and craft etc. (sometimes with reading) in the afternoon before play time and singing, poetry and story after'.

Teacher C   Pattern 2; 2nd year class

'There are three groups — green, blue and red; these are randomly selected and so of mixed ability. Each day begins with learning a reading page. On Tuesdays, Wednesdays and Thursdays there are three activity periods per day during which the groups rotate round four activities — number, reading, writing and choosing. On Mondays there is no group work and we concentrate on reading, writing, news and sounds. Fridays are for finishing off work and individual discussions'.

Teacher D   Pattern 2; transitionally grouped 1st and 2nd year class

'Maths, art and writing are done on a rotating basis by mixed ability groups. When the group has completed these three basic elements they are allowed to choose'.

Teacher E   Pattern 2; 1st year class

'There are six groups arranged by age. The day is based on three activity periods and during each two groups are doing maths, two groups are writing, and two groups are engaged in word building. After play in the afternoon the children have a free activity time'.

Teacher F   Pattern 2/3; vertically grouped class

'Initially each group is started on a particular activity. Then on movement to other activities is determined individually, sometimes by the child and sometimes by the teacher'.

Teacher G   Pattern 2/3; vertically grouped class

'There are three groups divided by age: top, middle, bottom. Each group is allotted different tasks at the beginning of the day, *e.g.* top — number, middle — writing, bottom — creative; each group works at its own level. After the first task is done, individual work occurs as decided by the teacher'.

Teacher H   Pattern 3; vertically grouped class

'Each child is expected to do some writing, number and reading every day. The rest of the day the children may choose their activity'.

Teacher I   Pattern 3; vertically grouped class

'Each child is expected to do some mathematics, reading, writing and creative activity each day, depending on the time available'.

Teacher J   Pattern 3; vertically grouped class
'Teacher's expectations: reading every day; maths, writing and other activities on most days; craft at least twice a week; physical activities four times a week'.

Teacher K   Pattern 3; vertically grouped class
'Everybody is required to do some maths, writing and or practical activity every day. The children's names are on a board and they put a piece of coloured plasticine beside their names when each task is completed'.

Teacher L   Pattern 3; 3rd year infants and 1st year juniors class
'Each child has a personal record sheet which he has to complete each day. It shows whether he has done: writing, number, reading aloud, phonic work, creative writing and other activities'.

Teacher M   Pattern 3; 2nd year class
'Each child must do basic skills every day. Teacher keeps a tick book and decides on today's activities for each child on the basis of what was done yesterday'.

Teacher N   Pattern 3; vertically grouped class
'Number, writing and reading are done every day, except that there is flexibility — if the child is deeply involved in something he can spend all day at it'.

Teacher O   Pattern 3; vertically grouped class
'Writing and number are expected each day, but not rigidly; if something else crops up this takes precedence'.

Teacher P   Pattern 3; transitionally grouped 1st and 2nd year class
'By the end of the day some work is expected — either writing or maths, sometimes both'.

Teacher Q   Pattern 3; vertically grouped class
'One good piece of maths or writing per day preferred if there is not enough time to do both'.

Teacher R   Pattern 3; vertically grouped class
'Three pieces of writing and of number required per week'.

Teacher S   Pattern 3; transitionally grouped 1st and 2nd year class
'Flexible pattern with no rules. If a child is doing something he is interested in, he is allowed to carry on'.

Later in the report, under the curriculum headings, the expectations of teachers are reported in some detail. Table 50 gives a summary of these.

Table 50   *'What are Your Curriculum Requirements for Younger and Older Infants?'*

each number shows the percentage of teachers saying 'Yes'	younger infants	older infants
expect all or nearly all of the children to **talk** individually with the teacher and to exchange a few sentences of conversation	83%	83%
expect all of the children to do some **mathematics** on at least four days in the week	69%	83%
expect all of the children to do some **writing** on at least four days in the week	81%	90%
expect all of the children to **read** aloud to an adult on at least three days in the week	76%	79%

N (younger infants) = 239 teachers; N (older infants) = 264 teachers. The first question did not distinguish between the two groups, hence 83% is given for both. Items in logical order.

We asked if any kind of regular assistance was available in the classroom and suggested seven possibilities. Table 51 shows the percentages of teachers getting different kinds of assistance. Of the seven kinds of assistance suggested, 24 per cent had three or more, 34 per cent had two, 29 per cent had one, and 12 per cent had no assistance at all.

Table 51   *Teachers Obtaining Regular Assistance is the Classroom*

percentage of teachers indicating that they
have the regular assistance of:

qualified infant helper or nursery nurse	42%
parent or other unpaid adult	50%
other teacher	28%
secondary school pupil	24%
student nursery nurse	20%
student teacher once a week	16%
unqualified infant helper	4%

N = 281 infant teachers. Items in rank order.

'Work' and 'play' are words that are very significant to infant teachers and so we asked 'Do you distinguish between 'work' and 'play' where work means the basic skills of the 3Rs?' Although some teachers expressed dissatisfaction with the wording of the question, all but 1 per cent answered; 48 per cent said 'Yes' and 51 per cent said 'No'. We then asked of those who had replied 'Yes', 'Do you expect "work" to take place mainly in the morning and "play" 'mainly in the afternoon?' One third replied 'Yes'.

The report now turns to the different areas of the curriculum.

Mathematics

Under this heading was included any activity where the main aim is to develop mathematical concepts and skills; instruction, work cards, exercises, practical mathematics, mental arithmetic, table recitation, etc.

We asked teachers how often they expected their children to engage in mathematical work. The replies are given in Table 52.

Table 52   *Teachers' Expectations in Mathematics*

each number shows the percentage of teachers saying 'Yes'	younger infants	older infants
'everybody to do some mathematics every day'	49%	62%
'everybody to do some mathematics at least on 4 days in every 5'	20%	21%
'everybody to do some mathematics regularly, but no daily requirement'	25%	15%
'mathematics to be done as appropriate with no regular requirement'	6%	2%

N (younger infants) = 239 teachers; N (older infants) = 264 teachers.
Items in logical order

We asked about the amount of time spent on mathematics, as shown in Table 53.

Table 53   *'When a Child does Mathematics, How Long Would You Expect Him to Spend on it During a Day?'*

each number shows the percentage of teachers saying 'Yes'	younger infants	older infants
'up to 15 minutes per day'	39%	3%
'between 15 and 30 minutes per day'	40%	42%
'between 30 and 45 minutes per day'	7%	38%
'more than 45 minutes per day'	2%	5%
'impossible to answer'	12%	12%

N (younger infants) = 239 teachers, N (older infants) = 264 teachers.
Items in logical order

Footnote   *The interpretation of 'younger' and 'older' was left to the respondents. 15 per cent of the teachers felt they had no 'younger infants' and 4 per cent that they had no 'older infants'.

In what ways do infants spend their time on mathematics? We asked this question separately for younger and older infants, but, since the replies for both were very similar, the figures given in Table 54 are combined. The table shows clearly that individual work with apparatus and with questions devised by the teacher is the most common approach. Group work and to a less extent class work is used by some teachers for some of the time. Commercial work cards and text books are used rarely.

There was a difference in the replies for younger and older children in the case of 'working individually from questions written on home made cards or worksheets'. Three times as many of the older children spend 'nearly all or most of the time' on this activity. This is to be expected; they are more likely to be able to read!

We asked whether the syllabus in mathematics, meaning a list of content and skills, was mainly the teacher's own, or whether it had been drawn up for the school. Three quarters of the teachers indicated that they were using their own syllabus and one quarter that they were following a school one.

Only three teachers' source books were widely cited. Fletcher's 'Mathematics for Schools' 43 per cent, 'Nuffield Mathematics' 17 per cent and Frobisher and Gloyn's 'Infants Learn Mathematics' 5 per cent.

Language

Under this heading was included any activity where the main aim is to promote language skills, *i.e.* talking, listening, reading aloud, reading silently, writing, comprehension, spelling, handwriting, etc.

Teachers were asked 'Do you have any deliberate procedures for promoting spoken language beyond every-day class discussion and conversation?' This was an open-ended question without prompting. Of the 281 infant teachers, 18 per cent cited drama, 11 per cent tape recordings made by the children, 8 per cent puppet work, and 4 per cent reported

Table 54   *'In What Ways do Your Children Spend their Time on Mathematics?'*

each line shows the percentages of teachers giving the answers:	'nearly all or most of the time	'some of the time	'a little or none of the time'
working individually with mathematical apparatus	25%	60%	15%
working individually from questions written in each child's book	23%	42%	35%
working individually from questions written on home made cards/ worksheets	22%	45%	33%
working as a group with mathematical apparatus or games etc	7%	62%	31%
working as a group orally with the teacher	4%	58%	38%
working individually from questions in class text books	4%	9%	87%
working as a class orally with the teacher	3%	30%	67%
working individually from questions on commercial workcards or kits	1%	11%	88%
working individually from questions on chalkboard or poster	0%	6%	94%

N = 281 infant teachers. Horizontal rows total 100%.
Items listed in rank order of first column

that they arrange group discussions in the classroom. Also 6 per cent indicated that they paid attention to the spoken language development of particular children in need. A variety of other answers were given, which amounted to variants of class discussion — children discussing objects brought in, news time, discussion of television, etc. Although 98 per cent had indicated in an earlier question (see Table 44) that there was regular class talk, 44 per cent had no answer to the enquiry into deliberate spoken language procedures other than every-day discussion and conversation.

We asked about the expectations for written work which teachers had. Scribble under a picture that is meaningful to the child was included as writing. Table 55 gives the results.

Table 55   *'What are Your Expectations for Each Child in Terms of Writing?'*

each number shows the percentage of teachers saying 'Yes'	younger infants	older infants
'everybody to do some writing every day'	65%	76%
'everybody to do some writing at least 4 days in every 5'	16%	14%
'everybody to do some writing regularly but no daily requirements'	15%	9%
'writing to be done as appropriate with no regular requirements'	4%	1%

N (younger infants) = 239 teachers; N (older infants) = 264 teachers. Items in logical order

We asked about the methods used for helping younger children to write. Table 56 gives the findings. Clearly the predominant approach is one in which the child draws a picture, talks to his teacher about it, she writes a description next to the picture and the child first traces on top of the teacher's writing, and later copies the teacher's writing. Some teachers described these two procedures as 'stage 1' and 'stage 2'; others stressed the importance of the child reading back to his teacher what he has written. In the table 'other' sometimes refers to variations of the listed items, such as copying on a separate sheet, or in a phrase book; 3 per cent of the teachers referred to the use of handwriting patterns from pattern cards or pattern books, and 1 per cent referred to each of the following : copying words from blackboard, tracing with the finger tactile cards, tracing letters in the air and tracing letters in sand.

Table 56   *'How Often do you Use these Methods for Younger Children Learning to Write?'*

each line shows the percentages of teachers giving the answers:	'nearly all or most of the time	'some of the time	'a little or none of the time'
child draws picture, teacher writes description given by child, child **copies** teacher's writing	47%	47%	6%
child draws picture, teacher writes description given by child, child **traces** on top of teacher's writing	28%	37%	35%
child **copies** letters and or words on a **sheet prepared** by teacher	8%	34%	58%
child traces letters and or words on **sheet prepared** by teacher	2%	26%	72%
other	5%	34%	61%

N = 239 infant teachers with 'younger' children. Horizontal rows total 100%. Items in rank order of first column

From where do children obtain the spelling of new words? The results of asking this are given in Table 57 and show how much this centres on the teacher herself.

Table 57   *'When your Older Children are Writing, from Where do they obtain the Spelling of New Words?'*

each line shows the percentages of teachers giving the answers:	'nearly all or most of the time	'some of the time	'a little or none of the time'
from teacher or other adults	50%	48%	2%
from picture dictionaries and other materials prepared by teacher	23%	65%	12%
from printed reference sources	6%	51%	43%
from other children	0%	28%	72%

N = 264 infant teachers with 'older children'. Horizontal rows total 100%. Items in rank order of first column.

We asked, 'Is your syllabus or policy for written language mainly your own or mainly the school's?' 83 per cent said that it was mainly their own; 17 per cent mainly the school's.

Very few infant teachers use class textbooks or commercial work cards for English. Table 58 lists the five books mentioned by 2 per cent and more of the respondents.

Table 58   *English Language Class Textbooks etc. in Common Use*

title and author or publisher		% of teachers mentioning
Ladybird Workcards		6%
'Sound Sense'	Tansley	5%
'Now to Measure'	Bromley	3%
'Read, Write and Remember'	Milburn	3%
'SRA Reading Laboratories'	SRA	2%

N = 281 infant teachers. '2%' or more listed. Items in rank order.

Clearly the various work books which link with reading schemes, such as Pirate Workbooks, One, Two, Three and Away Workbooks, Happy Venture Workbooks, etc. are not popular; these were each mentioned by not more than 1 per cent of the teachers.

It is also the case that very few of these teachers use any teacher's source books for language work. No book was cited by more than 1 per cent of the respondents.

As with other subjects we asked about the teachers' expectations in terms of reading and these are given in Table 59.

Table 59   *'What are your Expectations for Each Child in Terms of Reading?'*

each number shows the percentage of teachers saying 'Yes'	younger infants	older infants
everybody to read aloud to an adult every day	34%	34%
everybody to read aloud to an adult at least 3 days in every 5	42%	44%
everybody to read aloud to an adult at least 2 days in every 5	8%	9%
everybody to read aloud to an adult regularly but no daily requirement	12%	12%
reading to be done as appropriate with no regular requirement	4%	1%

N (younger infants) = 239 teachers; N (older infants) = 264 teachers. Items in logical order.

I.t.a. is used by only 2 per cent of the teachers.

The next question was adapted from one asked in the national survey for the Bullock Report. We asked about five different approaches to the learning of reading, in terms of how often they are used. The word recognition method known as 'look and say' is clearly the one most commonly used by these teachers.

Table 60   *'How Often do you Use these Methods for Younger Children Learning to Read?'*

each line shows the percentages of teachers giving the answers:	'nearly all or most of the time	'some of the time	'a little or none of the time'
look and say (word recognition)	65%	32%	3%
Phonic 1 (letter sounds digraphs and diphthongs)	22%	48%	30%
sentence method	5%	18%	77%
Phonic 2 (based on syllables)	2%	26%	72%
alphabetic analysis (letter names)	2%	20%	78%

N = 239 infant teachers with 'younger' children. Horizontal rows total 100%. Items listed in rank order of first column.

Table 61   *Reading Schemes in Common Use*

title and author(s) or publisher		% of teachers mentioning
'Ladybird Key Words Reading Scheme'	Murray	62%
The Griffin Pirate Stories	McCullagh	56%
'One, Two, Three and Away'	McCullagh	52%
'Gay Way Reading Scheme'	Boyce	43%
'Dominoes'	Glyn	19%
'Through the Rainbow'	Bradburne	18%
'Racing to Read'	Tansley & Nicholls	15%
'Reading with Rhythm'	Taylor, Jenny & Ingleby	14%
'Janet and John'	O'Donnell and Munro	13%
'Folk Tales'	Clarke	12%
'Kathy and Mark'	O'Donnell and Munro	10%
'Sparks'	Blackie	10%
'Happy Trio Reading Scheme'	Gray, Monroe and Artley	8%
'Breakthrough to Literacy'	Mackay, Thompson, Schaub	7%
'Gay Colour Books'	Williamson	7%
'Nippers'	Berg	7%
'Link Up'	Reid	6%
'Minibooks'	Collins	6%
'Language in Action'	Morris	5%
'Beacon Readers'	Fassett	4%
'Early to Read'	Tansley & Nicholls	4%
'Happy Venture Reading Scheme'	Schonell	4%
'Bangers and Mash'	Groves	4%
'Monsters'	Blance and Cook	3%

N = 281 infant teachers. '3%' or more listed. Items in rank order.

We asked whether the teacher's reading policy was mainly her own or mainly the school's design; 67 per cent said that it was their own.

All of the teachers interviewed used one or more graded reading schemes. Table 61 lists the reading schemes mentioned by 3 per cent and more of the respondents and Table 62 shows how many schemes different teachers use.

Table 62 *Numbers of Commercial Reading Schemes Used by Teachers*

number of reading schemes cited	1	2	3	4	5	6	7	8 plus
percentage of teachers in each set	7%	6%	12%	19%	16%	11%	8%	15%

N = 281 infant teachers. Row totals 94%; 6% used schemes but did not give details.

Integrated Studies or Topic Work

The infant school curriculum is not easy to analyze. What is the most appropriate label for the kind of activity carried on in most, if not all, infant classrooms, in which the teacher arouses interest in a particular matter and this serves as a starting point for discussion, writing, art and craft work and sometimes for number and even physical education? In the interviews we called it 'Integrated Studies etc' and explained what we meant with these words.. 'This includes activities carried out individually, in groups, or as a class, on topics or interests, for example 'Dinosaurs', 'People that Help Us', 'Goose Fair', 'Vegetables' etc.' All but 1 per cent of the teachers responded to the questions under this heading.

The choice of topics or interests is, almost invariably, left to the individual teacher. Only 1 per cent of our respondents indicated that they were working to a school scheme of work.

We asked for the titles of interests already studied during the current year, in progress, or planned, and this resulted in a list of 445 items, which is set out in Appendix 3. Table 63 gives the interests mentioned by 10 or more teachers.

Table 63   *The Most Popular Interests Mentioned by Infant Teachers*

title	% of teachers mentioning	title	% of teachers mentioning
'Christmas'	56%	'Ourselves'	6%
'Goose Fair'	41%	'Sea'	6%
'Colours'	38%	'Transport'	6%
'Bonfire Night/ Guy Fawkes'	33%	'People that help us'	6%
'Hallowe'en/witches'	32%	'Weather'	6%
'Animals/pets'	25%	'Weighing'	6%
'Seasons/months'	22%	'Senses'	6%
Topics from stories	20%	'Sounds'	6%
'Shapes'	19%	'Farms'	5%
'Jubilee'*	17%	'Money'	5%
'Autumn'	16%	'Shining things'	5%
'Time'	14%	'Growth'	5%
Letters (*e.g.* 'B') or sounds	14%	Other countries (*e.g.* 'France')	4%
'Spring'	11%	'Families'	4%
'Winter'	11%	'Holidays'	4%
'Houses/homes'	10%	'Eskimoes'	4%
'Water'	10%	'Pirates'	4%
'Measuring'	9%	'Flight'	4%
'Shopping'	9%	'Hibernation'	4%
'Harvest'	7%	'Hats'	4%
Numbers (*e.g.* '3')	8%	'Seaside'	4%
'Dinosaurs/dragons'	6%	'Snow'	4%
'Easter'	6%		

N = 281 infant teachers. *Teachers were interviewed during terms 1 and 2 of 1976/7; Queen Elizabeth II's Silver Jubilee was in term 3. '4%' or more listed. Items in rank order

Few of the teachers interviewed seemed to have an overall plan for the interests to be developed during the year; 50 per cent of the teachers questioned in term 1 were not able to give any indication of interests for the next two terms, but 21 per cent did have provisional plans for all three terms of the year. Of the latter it was noticeable that in nearly every case fewer interests were mentioned for succeeding terms, which indicates that in addition to planned items, other spontaneous interests would arise. Some examples of teachers' plans for the year are given in Table 64; they illustrate the way in which different interests develop in different classrooms and how some teachers try to achieve a balance between geographic, historical, scientific and everyday interests.

Table 64   *Five Examples of Interests Planned for the Year*

	Term 1	Term 2	Term 3
Teacher T Transitional grouping 1st/2nd years	'Yellow' 'People who care' 'Rough and smooth' 'Water'	'Things that fly' 'Blue' 'Homes' 'Children and growing'	'Shiny things' 'Pets'
Teacher U Transitional grouping 2nd/3rd years	'Nottingham' 'Length' 'Autumn' 'Harvest' 'Shiny' 'Hallowe'en' 'Christmas' 'Shape' 'Bravery'	'Volcanoes and rocks' 'Capacity' 'Blue' 'Jesus' life' 'Time'	'Birds' 'Mass' 'Money' 'London'
Teacher V Age grouping 3rd years	'Sea' 'Goose Fair' 'Autumn 'Hallowe'en' 'Bonfire Night'	'Weather' 'Spring' 'Dinosaurs'	'Insects' 'Summer'
Teacher W Vertical grouping 1st/2nd/3rd	'Autumn' 'Colours' 'Christmas' 'Winter'	'Water' 'Spring' 'The Farm'	'Ships' 'The Sea' 'Summer'
Teacher X Vertical grouping 1st/2nd/3rd	'Bears' 'Hats' 'Brushes' 'Trees' 'Homes' 'Bonfire Night'	'Water' 'Shape' 'Paper'	'Symmetry' 'Black and White'

The number of interests developed during a term varies widely from classroom to classroom. Table 65 gives the results of a count of the replies collected in term 2 (January to March) of the number of interests reported to have been used in term 1.

Table 65   *Numbers of Topics Developed in One Term by Different Teachers*

number of 'topics' developed during the autumn term	1	2	3	4	5	6	7 plus
percentage of teachers using each number of 'topics'	8%	12%	18%	10%	21%	10%	21%

N = 156 infant teachers. Row totals 100%

Who decides what the 'interest' to work on shall be? This depends to some extent on whether the activity is to be carried out by the class, or by groups or by children working individually. We asked whether teacher or children choose in terms of these three patterns of working. Table 66 gives the data which this question revealed.

How long do these interests last? Table 67 shows that activities lasting up to half a term are the most common.

We asked about books used by either teacher or children. The MacDonald 'Starters' series was mentioned by 18 per cent of the respondents and Ladybird books by 5 per cent. The Schools Council 'Science 5 - 13' series was cited by 4 per cent. Otherwise hardly any books were referred to.

Art and Craft

This was included under the heading of 'Integrated Studies etc'. Teachers were asked to indicate how much of the time spent on art and craft activities is devoted to a list of nine items. Table 68 gives the rank order of time spent on these.

We asked what other art and craft activities take place. Answers included : dough shaping, knitting, marbling,

Table 66   *Who Chooses the Activities of 'Integrated Studies'?*

this shows the percentages of teachers giving the answers:	'nearly all or most of the time'	'some of the time'	'a little or none of the time'
'teacher chosen class activities'	23%	46%	30%
'teacher chosen group activities'	18%	55%	26%
'children chosen individual activities'	14%	59%	26%
'teacher chosen individual activities'	9%	49%	41%
'children chosen class activities'	4%	46%	49%
'children chosen group activities'	2%	47%	50%

N = 281 infant teachers. Horizontal rows total 99%; 1% gave no answer. Items in rank order of first column.

Table 67   *'Length of Time Spent on 'Integrated Studies' Interests*

this shows the percentages of teachers giving the answers:	'nearly all or most of the time'	'some of the time'	'a little or none of the time'
'activities lasting no more than a half term'	53%	30%	15%
'activities lasting no more than a week'	11%	54%	33%
'activities lasting longer than a half term'	3%	9%	86%
'activities lasting no more than one day'	2%	28%	68%

N = 281 infant teachers. Horizontal rows total 98%; 2% gave no answer. Items in rank order of first column.

mobiles, montage, mosaics, nails and string work, paper folding, papier mache, plasticene, printing, puppets, rubbings, scissor work, soft toys, wax resist.

Table 68   *Art and Craft Activities: Rank Order of Time Spent on Nine Items:*

1	painting
2	collage
3	drawing
4	model making
5	clay work
6	needlework
7	cooking
8	fabric dyeing
9	woodwork

N = 281 infant teachers. Note: 'other' scored 10 in the rank order and examples of these activities are listed in the text.

Other Resources

We asked whether the items of Table 69 were available in classrooms. The question was posed with the items in alphabetical order, but it is given here in rank order of 'always'.

Music

The extent to which the classes of the teachers interviewed engage in musical activities is shown in Table 70. Singing is the most prevalent.

We asked if music teaching was carried out by a colleague rather than by the class teacher herself; 25 per cent of the classes were taught singing, 17 per cent made music and 8 per cent listened to music with a teacher other than the class teacher. A regular visiting pianist plays for 72 per cent of the classes, while the remaining 28 per cent are played to by their own teachers. 17 per cent of the teachers reported that they play the guitar to their classes and also 17 per cent play the recorder.

Table 69   *Art, Craft and Play Resources. 'To what Extent are these Resources Available for your Class'*

each line shows the percentages of teachers answering:	'always available'	'sometimes available'	'not available'
painting	95%	5%	0%
collage	87%	13%	0%
small bricks	84%	8%	8%
wendy house/home corner	81%	6%	13%
dressing up materials	78%	12%	10%
big bricks	73%	16%	11%
large construction materials	44%	20%	36%
water trough	43%	42%	15%
sand trough (dry)	39%	43%	17%
clay	32%	54%	14%
sand trough (wet)	26%	50%	24%
shop	21%	58%	21%
woodwork bench	14%	35%	51%
puppets	14%	59%	27%
cooking	11%	79%	10%

N = 281 infant teachers. Horizontal row totals 100%.
Items in rank order of first column

Table 70   *Ways in which Children Spend Their Time on Music*

each line shows the percentages of teachers giving the answers:	'nearly all or most of the time'	'some of the time'	'a little or none of the time'
singing	71%	26%	1%
making music	3%	53%	42%
listening to music	0%	37%	61%

N = 281 infant teachers. Horizontal rows total 98%; no reply from 2%.
Items in rank order of first column.

Of the teachers making music with their classes, more or less all engage in rhythmic percussion, 26 per cent in tuned or melodic percussion and 11 per cent use recorders. We asked if teachers expected to make some simple musical instruments with their children during the year and 80 per cent said 'Yes'.

We asked for the name of any particular books used by the teacher and items mentioned by five and more people are listed in Table 71.

Table 71   *Music and Singing Books Used by Teachers*

title and author, etc.		% of teachers mentioning
'Apusskidu'	Harrop (editor)	14%
'Okki Tokki Unga'	Harrop (editor)	9%
'Someone's Singing, Lord'	Black	4%
'High Road of Song'	Fletcher and Davidson	3%
'Time and Tune' pamphlets	BBC	2%
'Carol Gaily Carol'	Harrop (editor)	2%
'Singing Together'	BBC	2%

N = 281 infant teachers. '2%' or more listed. Items in rank order

Table 72   *Popular Music for Class Listening*

title and composer		% of teachers mentioning
Classical		
'Peter and the Wolf'	Prokofiev	11%
'The Planets' Suite'	Holst	8%
'Carnival of the Animals'	Saint-Saens	5%
'The Sorcerer's Apprentice'	Dukas	5%
'Peer Gynt Suite'	Grieg	3%
'Pictures from an Exhibition'	Mussorgsky	2%
'Danse Macabre'	Saint-Saens	2%
Film, Pop, Folk Music, etc.		
'The Ugly Duckling'	(Danny Kaye/ Hans Andersen)	2%
'Spinners'		2%

N = 281 infant teachers. '2%' or more listed. Items in rank order.

The teachers were asked whether they used ideas from any well-known method of teaching music as the basis for their work. Few said 'Yes'; of the 281 teachers, 4 per cent cited Orff and 2 per cent Dankworth.

Where teachers played recorded music to their pupils we asked for the titles of three recent pieces. Items mentioned by five or more teachers are listed in Table 72.

Physical Education

This was taken to mean all of the activities such as apparatus work, movement, out-of-door activities, swimming and games, where the main aim is to promote the physical co-ordination of the body, body-awareness and the acquisition of social and physical skills.

We asked 'Of the time which your class spends on physical education in school time, can you indicate how much is devoted to these six activities?' The items and collated replies are given in Table 73.

Table 73   *Ways in which Children Spend their Time in*
            Physical Education

each line shows the percentages of teachers giving the answers:	'nearly all or most of the time'	'some of the time'	'a little or none of the time'
large apparatus	28%	64%	7%
floorwork	7%	71%	21%
small apparatus (hoops, etc)	2%	70%	27%
music and movement/ dance	1%	74%	24%
swimming	1%	23%	75%*
team games	0%	14%	83%

*N = 281 infant teachers. Horizontal rows total 99%; 1% gave no answer. Items in rank order of first column. *swimming 'none of the time' 54%*

Only 8 per cent of the teachers worked to a school syllabus for physical education. Table 74 gives a listing of source books for teachers in physical education, as reported by five or more teachers.

Table 74   *Teachers' Source Books in Physical Education in Common Use*

title and author(s) or publisher		% of teachers mentioning
'PE is Fun'	Brown*	16%
'Movement Education for Infants'	ILEA	10%
'Physical Education Programme for Juniors'	Mitchell*	2%
'Creative Dance in the Primary School'	Russell	2%
'Games and Sports'	Wise	2%
'Gymnastics'	Buckland	2%
'PE in the Primary School'	Bilbrough and Jones	2%

N = 281 infant teachers. '2%' or more listed. Items in rank order.
*Booklets by Notts LEA advisers.

We asked about children with physical problems. 'Other than any children recognized as 'physically handicapped', are there children in your class with poor muscular co-ordination, poor posture, or flat feet?' We did not enquire into how many such children there were, but just whether there were any. The presence of at least one child with poor muscular co-ordination was reported by 41 per cent of the teachers, of at least one with poor posture by 3 per cent and of flat feet by 13 per cent.

We asked for an estimate of the number of half-days during the school year when the class would be out of school on a visit during school time 'mainly for physical education objectives'. In many cases this would mean swimming. While 66 per cent said 'none', 27 per cent reported that they would be on such visits on ten or more occasions during the year.

The report now turns to some general matters of teaching.

Marking
We asked three questions about marking, which are set

out, with the answers given, in Tables 75, 76 and 77. We gave a broad meaning to 'mark' : 'any form of response to your pupils' written work, such as spoken comment, written comment, numerical mark, etc.'

Table 75   *'How Much of Your Pupils' Writing and Mathematics Do You Mark?'*

percentages of teachers giving the answers:	'all or nearly all'	'most'	'some'
	94%	4%	1%

N = 281 infant teachers. Row totals to 99%; 1% gave no answer

Table 76   *'Of the Writing and Mathematics That You Mark, Please Estimate How Much is Marked in the Presence of, or in the Absence of, the Pupil'*

percentage of teachers giving the answers:	'all or most'	'some'	'a little or none'
'marked with the pupil present'	93%*	6%	1%
'marked without the pupil but discussed individually with him when returned'	2%	10%	88%
'marked without the pupil and without individual discussion on return'	1%	2%	97%

*N = 281 infant teachers. Horizontal rows total 100%. Items in rank order of first column. *81% said 'all or nearly all'.*

Table 77 *'Which of These Forms of Response to Individual Children Do You Use and How Often'*

percentages of teachers giving the answers:	'frequently'	'sometimes'	'rarely or never'
'extended spoken comment' *eg* discussion of work	68%	29%	3%
'tick'	68%	27%	5%
'brief spoken comment' *eg* 'well done'	45%	50%	5%
'brief written comment' *eg* 'neat'	10%	44%	46%
'star'	8%	20%	72%
'other'*	7%	15%	78%
'extended written comment' *eg* commentary on work	2%	14%	84%
'house point'	1%	1%	98%
'numerical mark' *eg* 5/10	0%	1%	99%
'grade' *eg* 'C'	0%	0%	100%

N = 281 infant teachers. Horizontal rows total 100%.
*Items in rank order of first column. *'other' — see below.*

A variety of other responses were given. Happy or sad faces, rapidly drawn by the teacher, were mentioned by 7 per cent of the respondents; 4 per cent used 'showing work to the rest of the class' as a reward, while each of the following were mentioned by 2 per cent : showing to another teacher or head', entering the child's name in the 'commendation' book, or giving sweets. A novel variant on the awarding of stars was mentioned by one teacher : 'star stuck on child, not on book'.

Record Keeping and Destiny of Completed Work

We asked about records of the work done by the class or by groups within the class, and about notes of individual children's difficulties and successes. The replies are shown in Table 78.

Table 78   *Records. 'In Which Subjects Do You Keep Written Records of the Work Done by the Class or by Groups Within the Class?' 'Do you Keep Notes of Individual Children's Difficulties and Successes?'*

the table shows the percentages of teachers saying 'Yes. I keep this kind of record'

	notes of work done by class or group	notes of individual's difficulties and successes
Mathematics	82%	80%
Reading	80%	87%
Topic/		
Integrated Studies	70%	53%
Written Language	69%	77%
Art and Craft	52%	61%
Physical Education	43%	64%
Music	42%	45%
Spoken Language	39%	70%

N = 281 infant teachers. 99% responded. Items in rank order of first column.

What records, if any, do infant teachers keep of the social and emotional development of individual children? Of the 281 teachers in this survey 78 per cent reported that they keep thumbnail sketches of their children and 10 per cent use a check list record.

We asked what happens to children's work when it is completed and asked teachers to reply in terms of seven possibilities. The replies are shown in Tables 79 and 80.

Table 79 *'What Happens to Children's Written Work when it is Completed?'*

each line shows the percentages of teachers giving the answers:	'always or frequently'	'sometimes'	'rarely or never
stored in folder/tray etc until end of school year	62%	15%	23%
kept for record purposes	47%	30%	23%
stored in folder/tray etc until end of term	47%	17%	36%
displayed on wall	40%*	53%	7%
taken home	20%	35%	45%
thrown away during term	1%	16%	83%
thrown away immediately	0%	2%	98%

*N = 281 infant teachers. Horizontal rows total 100%. Items in rank order of first column. *39% 'frequently'.*

We also asked what criteria teachers use when choosing work for display on the classroom wall. How often is it motivation of the individual child, and is a cross-section of all work displayed or the best work from the class? The replies are shown in Table 81.

Children with Special Needs

We asked each teacher whether there were children (one or more) in her class whom she considered to be seriously lacking in mathematics, spoken language, written language or reading. The definition of 'seriously lacking' was left to the individual teacher's judgment. Only 1 per cent of the 281

Table 80   *'What Happens to Children's Art and Craft Work when it is completed?'*

each line shows the percentages of teachers giving the answers:	'always or frequently'	'sometimes'	'rarely or never
displayed on wall	83%	17%	0%
taken home	47%	40%	13%
stored in folder/tray etc until end of term	9%	26%	65%
thrown away during term	7%	56%	36%
stored in folder/tray etc until end of school year	7%	18%	75%
kept for record purposes	5%	24%	71%
thrown away immediately	2%	24%	71%

N = 281 infant teachers. Horizontal rows total 100%. Items in rank order of first column.

Table 81   *'What Criteria Do You Apply When Choosing Work for Class Wall Display?'*

each line shows the percentages of teachers giving the answers:	'always or frequently'	'sometimes'	'rarely or never
motivation of individual child	62%	34%	4%
cross-section of all work	55%	35%	9%
best work from the class	17%	43%	40%

N = 281 infant teachers. Horizontal rows total 100%. Items in rank order of first column.

teachers declined to reply. Answers of 'Yes' were given as follows : spoken language 68 per cent, reading 63 per cent, written language 55 per cent, mathematics 51 per cent. As an open-ended question we asked what special provision, if any, was made for these children. 43 per cent of the teachers indicated that they enlisted the help of another teacher (head, deputy, fellow class teacher, community teacher, or remedial teacher). The help of speech therapists was mentioned by 16 per cent; another 5 per cent referred to nursery nurses.

Another question looked at the opposite end of the ability spectrum and asked 'Are there any very able children in your class who really need special work programmes in order to make the best use of their time in school?' Answers of 'Yes' were given by 29 per cent of the teachers. Most of them indicated that they tried to provide individual attention for these children.

A third question about children with special needs enquired about disruptive children. 'Are there any children in your class who are particularly disruptive in that they regularly interfere with the learning of other children?' 'Yes' was the reply of 35 per cent of the teachers. In reply to an open-ended question about any special arrangements made for these children, five major answers were made. 'Increase the supervision of the child' was the answer of 13 per cent of the teachers, 'provide special work' said 6 per cent and 5 per cent said each of 'extract the child from the class', 'isolate him in the class', and 'refer to child psychologist'.

Assembly

We asked each teacher what she did when her class attended assembly and offered four alternatives, of which respondents might tick some or all as appropriate. We also asked how many times in a term the teacher was likely to be responsible for assembly, including times when her class was providing it. The answers to these questions are in Tables 82 and 83.

Radio and Television Programmes Used in School

We enquired into the television and radio broadcasts used

Table 82   *'What Do You Do When your Class is at Assembly?'*

	% of teachers mentioning
'attend assembly'	68%
'prepare teaching, mark work, etc'	43%
'work with a small remedial group of children'	43%
'meet with other staff'	36%
'other'*	17%

N = 281 infant teachers. 'Other' was half 'prepare displays' and half 'work with group of children — not remedial'

Table 83   *'How Often Per Term are you Responsible for an Assembly (Including when your Class is Providing it)?'*

number of assemblies taken per term	none	1	2	3	4	5-9	10 plus
percentage of teachers in each set	22%	10%	19%	10%	8%	10%	20%

N = 281 infant teachers, but 1% gave no reply.

in school; only 18 per cent of the teachers made no regular use of these. On average each teacher uses just over two broadcasts per week, but such data is better expressed as in Table 84.

Table 84   *'How Many Television and Radio Programmes Does your Class Experience Regularly?'*

percentage of teachers replying:	'no programmes'	'1 programme'	'2 programmes'	'3 programmes'	'4 programmes'	'5 and more programmes'
radio	42%	29%	16%	8%	4%	1%
television	28%	35%	25%	6%	5%	1%
radio and television	18%	17%	23%	15%	15%	12%

N = 281 infant teachers. Horizontal rows total 100%.

Table 85 shows the programmes used by 2 per cent and more of the teachers.

Table 85   *Popular Radio and Television Broadcasts Used in Schools*

programme title	source	% of teachers using it
'Watch'	BBC TV	41%
'Let's Move'	BBC radio	19%
'Movement, Mime and Music'	BBC radio	18%
'Words and Pictures'	BBC TV	17%
'Seeing and Doing'	ITV	16%
'My World: Real Life'	ITV	14%
'Let's Join In'	BBC radio	14%
'Poetry Corner'	BBC radio	12%
'Time and Tune'	BBC radio	10%
'You and Me'	BBC TV	9%
'My World: Stories'	ITV	7%
'Stories and Rhymes'	BBC radio	7%
'Play School'	BBC TV	6%
'Time to Move'	BBC radio	6%
'Stop, Look and Listen'	ITV	5%
'It's Fun to Read'	ITV	5%
'Music Box'	BBC radio	5%
'Playtime'	BBC radio	4%
'Funny Folk'	Radio Nottingham	2%
'The Decayers'	Radio Nottingham	2%
'Look and Read'	BBC TV	2%

N = 281 infant teachers. Items in rank order. '2%' or more listed.

Of the total number of broadcasts received by the classes of the survey, 45 per cent were radio and 55 per cent television; 76 per cent were 'off-air' and 24 per cent recorded and played back later. Radio Nottingham broadcasts were used by 12 per cent of the teachers.

We asked whether programmes were 'central or peripheral to teaching'. The replies indicated that the teachers felt that 28 per cent of the programmes were central to their work. Printed materials were obtained for 55 per cent of the programmes.

Visits and Visitors

At least 80 per cent of the teachers organize visits for their

classes during the school year and during school time. We
asked 'What places have you visited with groups of children
during school time during the past twelve months?' Table 86
shows the number of visits in the year reported on by each
teacher and Table 87 lists the categories of places visited.

Table 86   *Number of Visits Made by Teachers with Children during
Previous Year*

number of visits	0	1	2	3	4	5	6 plus
percentage of teachers in each set	20%	13%	18%	15%	15%	9%	10%

N = 281 infant teachers. Row totals 100%

Table 87   *Places Visited by Teachers with Children During
Previous Year*

	% of times mentioned
parks, nature reservations, woodland, etc.	26%
places in the vicinity of the school (shops, post office, library, etc)	22%
places in Nottinghamshire (further afield than school)	16%
stately homes, castles, etc	11%
zoos	10%
cinemas, theatres, concerts	6%
places outside Nottinghamshire	3%
exhibitions	3%
churches and cathedrals	2%
museums	1%

*N = circa 700 visits. Column totals 100%. Items in rank order.
Note that there are difficulties in categorizing some items.*

We enquired about any 'visitors who have talked to or worked with your class during the past twelve months either in classroom or assembly'. The numbers of visitors received in different classrooms is given in Table 88 and a category list of some of the visitors in Table 89. Other visitors included the Lord Mayor of Nottingham, the Mayor of Gedling, a zoologist, a bee keeper, overseas visitors from Persia, India, Brazil and the U.S., a mother with ferrets, a window cleaner, and Santa Claus.

Table 88   *'Number of Visitors who have Talked to or Worked with the Class During the Previous Year'*

number of visitors	0	1	2	3	4	5	6 plus
percentage of teachers in each set	29%	21%	20%	12%	8%	5%	5%

N = 281 infant teachers. Row totals 100%

Table 89   *Category List of Some Visitors*

	% of teachers mentioning
Police	33%
Parent	8%
Clergy	7%
Road Safety Officer	6%
Nurse	6%
'Lollipop' Lady	6%
Puppet Show	4%
School Caretaker	4%
Theatre Group	4%
Red Cross	3%
Fireman	3%

N = 281 infant teachers. List is not additive. Items in rank order.

PART IV HEAD TEACHERS

Introduction

Fewer questions were asked of the headteachers. In total 114 were interviewed and some of the characteristics of the schools as reported by them are given in Table 90.

Table 90 *Some Characteristics of the Schools Surveyed*

type of school	primary	42%			
	infant	25%			
	junior	33%			
		100%			
design of teaching accommodation	classrooms only		63%		
	open plan only		6%		
	part classroom/part open plan		31%		
			100%		
number of teachers			primary	infant	junior
	2— 5 teachers		33%	10%	5%
	6—10 teachers		38%	87%	49%
	10—15 teachers		23%	3%	38%
	16—20 teachers		6%	0%	8%

N = 114 schools (48 primary, 29 infant, 37 junior)

The two previous parts of the report have shown that in this area there are few team teaching situations. Further information was gained from the heads by asking whether teachers were 'class teachers'(*i.e.* teachers who spend most or all of their time with their own classes), 'team teachers' (*i.e.* teachers working as a team of two, three or four, and in a shared space), 'floating teachers' (*i.e.* teachers who work across the school and who do not have a class or registration group of their own), or 'other' (usually meaning community teacher). The answers to this question are in Table 91. Overall 5 per cent of the teaching force are floating teachers.

Table 91   *Teaching Responsibilities of Teachers*

the percentages in this table refer to numbers of teachers

	primary	infant	junior
class teachers	85%	87%	86%
team teachers	7%	6%	6%
floating teachers	6%	3%	6%
other	2%	4%	2%
	100%	100%	100%

N = 977 teachers (390 primary, 198 infant, 389 junior)

It was surprising to find that of the seven schools described as 'open plan' only two were organized on a team teaching basis. Of the 6 per cent of teachers overall who are engaged in team teaching, one third are in 'classroom' schools, one third in 'open plan' schools and one third in 'part classroom/ part open-plan' schools.

Who Makes What Decisions

We enquired as to the extent to which the patterns of organization used in the schools are determined by head-teachers, or by individual teachers. Three statements were presented to the headteachers with the request that they tick which ever one seemed nearest to their own position. A distinction was made between the headteacher's approach to experienced and to inexperienced teachers. Table 92 gives the replies.

Table 92 *Headteacher's Influence on Patterns of Classroom Organization*

the % of heads ticking one of the following is shown		applies to experienced teachers	applies to inexperienced teachers
statement 'A'	'As headteacher I have described a pattern of classroom or team organization which I ask teachers to use'	13%	27%
statement 'B'	'As head teacher I have recommended a pattern of classroom or team organization but I leave the decision to the teachers'	36%	29%
statement 'C'	'As headteacher I expect individual teachers or teams to choose their own pattern of classroom organization'	49%	34%
no reply or alternative comment		2%	10%
		100%	100%

N = 114 headteachers

In general, the heads of infant schools were twice as likely to tick statement 'A' as the heads of junior schools.

As an open-ended question we asked for details of patterns of organization that are set, or recommended, by heads. The following extracts from the replies indicate the wide range of such patterns.

Head 'A'   11 teachers in classrooms; junior school
    'I draw up a skeleton time-table for use of hall and equipment, radio and TV, and for swimming. The teachers arrange their daily programme within this framework'.

Head 'B'   9 teachers in classrooms; junior school
    'I expect all teachers to do basic skills in the mornings and other activities in the afternoons'.

Head 'C'   12 teachers in classrooms; junior school
'The children throughout the school are set in ability groups for English, mathematics and reading. Reading groups are organized so that four classes form six groups'.

Head 'D'   8 teachers in classrooms; junior school
'I expect group organization, but with a fair amount of classwork to assist with control. Basic subjects are to be taught in ability groups; other subjects in mixed ability groups. I also expect adequate forward planning on a weekly basis'.

Head 'E'   10 teachers in classrooms; junior school
'Organization depends upon the subject and on the ability of the teacher. If there are disciplinary problems I recommend a fairly formal pattern as a temporary measure, leading to a more permanent pattern of a combination of children working in groups and of class method. There should be a class session daily for activities such as story, topic, discussion. Children with early reading problems are set across the classes and meet regularly'.

Head 'F'   8 teachers in part classrooms, part open-plan; primary school
'For inexperienced teachers I recommend starting with a rather formal style, class teaching orientated, and gradually move into group work on a rotating basis. For experienced teachers I recommend a mixture of class teaching, group work and individual assignments'.

Head 'G'   8 teachers in classrooms; junior school
'It is suggested that at the beginning of the year the children are taught 'formally' but that this pattern changes to group work and then to individually assigned work. This gives the children an idea of the standards required but gives them a free rein, if possible, by the end of the year'.

Head 'H'   8 teachers in classrooms; junior school
'I recommend a mixture of approaches. Classwork for music and P.E. etc. Group work within a class lesson for

mathematics. Rotating groups for other mathematics, art and creative writing'.

Head 'I'   6 teachers in classrooms; infant school
'I recommend group work based on mathematics, English topic and art on a rotating basis. Within these groups individual work'.

Head 'J'   3 teachers in classrooms; primary school
'Reading, writing and mathematics must be done every day, but the teachers can organize it as they wish'.

Head 'K'   2 teachers in classrooms; primary school
'We have a structured environment with children working at their own pace, sometimes in a group, sometimes as a class, and sometimes individually. Work is often based on centres of interest, with much apparatus. Assignment work and topics are usual. It may be best to be more formal early in the year'.

Head 'L'   11 teachers in classrooms; infant school
'This is the pattern which I ask all of my teachers to follow:

9.00 – 10.45	Creative, mathematical and English activities with special reference to the stimulation and development of children's interests and use of displays.
10.45 – 11.00	Assembly and prayers.
11.00 – 12.00	Quiet time. Discussions, poetry, music, demonstrations of practical mathematics, religious education. Preparations for afternoon activities.
1.30 – 2.45	Creative, mathematical and English activities.
2.45 – 3.00	Clearing away and discussion of next day's work and interests.
3.00 – 3.30	Story, music, poetry'.

Head 'M'   5 teachers in classrooms; infant school
'I expect all aspects of the curriculum to be integrated

with all ages working, either individually or in self-chosen groups, at self-chosen activities. On three days a week I take two services : for older children 10.30 to 11.00 and for younger children 11.00 to 11.25. At these times the teachers pair up and group the children according to ability for teaching points in language, mathematics and sometimes science or topic. Teachers also work in pairs, with both of their classes together, for movement, TV, swimming, music and some stories. Older children are expected to structure their own day. Children learn best through self-motivated activities, but it is the teachers' job to see that all the children are motivated in all the aspects of the curriculum'.

Who decides what is to be taught in school? For a number of subjects we asked, 'Who decides on the outline syllabus : head, a teacher with special responsibility for the subject, a group of staff or individual teachers?' The replies are given in Table 93. 'No answer' may mean that the answer was too complicated to fit into the structured responses, or, as in the case of 'topic' that the subject does not feature as such in the school's curriculum. It was left to the respondent to decide what is meant by 'outline'.

Table 93   *'Who Decides on the Outline Syllabuses?'*

	headteacher	group of staff	individual teachers	teacher with special responsibility	no answer
Mathematics	34%	46%	8%	6%	6%
Language (English)	32%	40%	16%	4%	8%
Physical Education	18%	27%	43%	7%	5%
Music	16%	28%	35%	11%	10%
Art and Craft	13%	21%	45%	4%	17%
Topic	10%	20%	34%	2%	34%

N = 114 headteachers. Horizontal rows total to 100%.
Items in rank order of first column

We also asked what responsibilities heads delegate to individual teachers, beyond the day-to-day teaching of their classes. Table 94 gives the percentages of positive replies to a list of 14 items.

Table 94   *Responsibilities Delegated to Individual Teachers*

	% of heads indicating that a teacher had been made responsible for this function
school library organizer	72%
language/reading/English consultant	67%
music consultant	61%
audio-visual aids consultant	54%
out-of-door activities organizer	54%
mathematics consultant	48%
art and craft consultant	47%
needlework consultant	37%
responsibility for infant part of school	36%
liaison with other schools	25%
science consultant	21%
responsibility for junior part of school	20%
tuck shop organizer	18%
responsibility for leading a teaching team	8%

N = 114 headteachers. Items in rank order

Transfer to Secondary Schools

We asked a number of questions of primary and junior school heads about the transfer of children at eleven plus to secondary schools. First we enquired into the number of secondary schools that each primary school feeds. In Table 95 an arbitary definition of 'feed' has been chosen; it means that 5 or more pupils were transferred to the secondary school in the summer of 1976.

Only a few children transfer from these schools to schools outside the state system; these children came from 16 per cent of the schools in the survey.

Table 95   *'How Many Secondary Schools does each Primary School Feed?'*

	% of primary schools
primary schools feeding 1 secondary school	42%
primary schools feeding 2 secondary schools	32%
primary schools feeding 3 secondary schools	17%
primary schools feeding 4 or more secondary schools	9%
	100%

N = 82 primary schools (JMI and Junior schools)
'Feed' means transfer 5 or more pupils in 1976

We asked several questions about the contacts between primary schools and the secondary schools whom they feed. Did the children have an opportunity to visit their secondary school as a group towards the end of their last year in primary school? Did any teachers from the secondary schools visit the primary school to meet the children who were transferring, or to discuss with the teachers any individual children who might have learning difficulties in the secondary school? The responses to these questions are given in the following tables.

Table 96   *'Did your Leaving Children have an Opportunity Towards the End of Last Year to Visit their Secondary Schools as a Group and to be Shown Around?'*

	% of primary schools
'Yes. All or nearly all of our children made a visit'	81%
'Yes. Most of our children made a visit'	13%
'Yes. Some of our children made a visit'	2%
'No. None of our children made a visit'	4%
	100%

N = 82 primary schools. 'All or nearly all' = 95—100%; 'Most' = 75—94%; 'Some' = 1—74%. This table (and the next two) is presented in a slightly different form to the way the question was asked.

Table 97   *'Did your Leaving Children Receive a Visit from Teachers of their Secondary Schools at the Primary School?'*

	% of primary schools
'Yes. All or nearly all of our children met visiting teachers'	57%
'Yes. Most of our children met visiting teachers'	24%
'Yes. Some of our children met visiting teachers'	8%
'No. None of our children had visiting teachers'	11%
	100%

N = 82 primary schools. Terms as defined in Table 96

Table 98   *'Did any Secondary School Teachers Discuss with the Primary School any Children who might have Learning Difficulties in the Secondary School?'*

	% of primary schools
'Yes. From the schools to where all or nearly all of our children transfer'	53%
'Yes. From schools to where most of our children transfer'	23%
'Yes. From schools to where some of our children transfer'	12%
'No'	12%
	100%

N = 82 primary schools. Terms as defined in Table 96

These answers indicate that for the majority of children transferring to secondary schools there have been some contacts between the two schools involved.

We also asked whether secondary schools had shown any interest or concern over the primary school curriculum. 'Did any secondary school teachers discuss the curriculum of the primary school last year in order to find out what is taught?' 63 per cent of the primary schools answered 'Yes' and 37 per cent said 'No'. 'Did any secondary school teachers discuss the curriculum of the primary school in order to try to influence some aspect of it?' In this case only 14 per cent said 'Yes' and 86 per cent 'No'. In the few cases where secondary teachers had sought to influence the primary school curriculum this was in mathematics and English.

Transfer from Infant to Junior Schools

Similar questions to those asked about transfer to secondary schools were asked of infant headteachers about the transfer of children to junior schools. The sample was, of course, much smaller and totals 29 infant schools. In general the impression is of close links between infant and junior schools, in terms of our questions.

Table 99 shows that most infant schools feed only one junior school. Of the 29 schools, none reported children moving out of the state system into private schools.

Table 99   *'How many Junior Schools does each Infant School Feed?*

	% of infant schools
infant school feeding 1 junior school	73%
infant school feeding 2 junior schools	24%
infant school feeding 3 junior schools	3%
	100%

N = 29 infant schools. 'Feed' means transfer 5 or more pupils in 1976

In all of the 29 schools the children leaving last year had an opportunity to visit their junior schools in groups to be shown around. Also, in every case bar two, visiting teachers from the junior schools talked to them at the infant school about the transfer. In every case except one teachers from the junior school discussed with the infant school staff any children who might have learning difficulties in the junior school.

How far have junior school teachers shown interest or concern about the infant school curriculum? 'Did any junior school teachers discuss the curriculum of the infant school in order to find out what is taught?'; 79 per cent of the infant heads said 'Yes' and 21 per cent 'No'. 'Did any junior school teachers discuss the curriculum of the infant school in order to try to influence some aspects of it?'; 24 per cent of the infant heads said 'Yes' and 76 per cent 'No'.

Links between Home and School

Heads were given a list of five kinds of opportunity for parents to meet teachers in order to discuss their children's work and progress, and asked which of these they provided. The replies are in Table 100.

Table 100   *'Which of these Opportunities for Parents to Meet Teachers to Discuss their Children's Work and Progress do you Provide?'*

	% of headteachers indicating 'Yes'
open evenings when parents are invited to the school and can see their child's teacher, headteacher and their child's work	88%
standing invitation to parents to request an interview to discuss their child's work and progress with the class teacher	85%
standing invitation to parents to request an interview to discuss their child's work and progress with the headteacher	82%
open days when parents are invited to the school and can see their child at work	59%
'open house' *ie* when parents have a permanent invitation to visit the school at any time and see their child at work	58%

N = 114 headteachers. Items in rank order

Many primary schools invite parents into school to give voluntary help. Only 9 per cent of our sample don't. Table

101 gives heads' estimates of numbers of parents giving voluntary help in school in a typical week.

Table 101   *'In a Typical Week how many Parents will be Giving Voluntary Help to the School?'*

number of parents	none	1-5	6-10	11-15	16 plus
% of schools in each set	9%	24%	31%	17%	19%

N = 114 headteachers. Row totals 100%

Where parents are giving help we asked what this was. Table 102 gives replies to seven items suggested. Other forms of assistance were also mentioned : making books, mounting pictures, clerical work, making classroom equipment, cutting paper, mixing paints, etc.

Table 102   *Voluntary Help given by Parents*

	% of headteachers indicating 'Yes'
accompanying school visits	82%
accompanying swimming parties	75%
needlework	65%
cooking	56%
hearing reading	54%
providing transport	43%*
assisting with games	23%*

*N = 114 headteachers. Items in rank order. *zero for infants*

One head made a number of points about her decision not to have parents working in school, as follows. 'I don't have any mothers in school to help because I believe it can confuse the children by introducing their home standard of behaviour into school. Also some mothers could never come in and their children might be upset by this, seeing other mothers and not their own. Also articulate mothers can try to run the job and get difficult over issues that arise. But I do have close relationships with parents; they are free to approach me at any time. I arrange to see them all individually to talk about their child's progress'.

We asked about the kind of information given to parents. In terms of written information, 85 per cent of the head-teachers send parents information on school administrative matters, 38 per cent on ways in which the parents might assist in the education of their children, and 25 per cent on what and how their children are taught. In terms of spoken information, 60 per cent provide talks for parents on what and how their children are taught.

Of the 114 schools, 39 per cent have 'an organization for parents and teachers'. Table 103 shows the function of these in terms of the answers given to a structured question.

Table 103   *'Where there is an Organization for Parents and Teachers Please Indicate the Extent to which its Function is Educational, Social or Fund-Raising'*

each line shows the % of heads replying	'mostly'	'in part'	'rarely/never'
social	25%	71%	4%
fund-raising	20%	71%	9%
educational	14%	61%	25%

N = 45 headteachers. Horizontal rows total 100%.
Items in rank order of first column

Full list of story books being read to junior classes at the time of interview. (Extension of Table 17).

Adams, R.	*Watership Down*
Adamson, J.	*Born Free*
Aesop	*Fables*
Aiken, J.	*A Necklace of Raindrops*
Ainsworth, R.	*Ten Tales of Shellover*
Andersen, H.	*Ugly Duckling*
Andersen, H.	*Fairy Tales*
Andrew, P.	*Ginger over the Wall*
Andrew, P.	*Una and Grubstreet*
Ashley, B.	*The Trouble with Donovan Croft*
Ballantyne, R.M.	*Coral Island*
Barrie, J.M.	*Peter Pan*
Barry, M.S.	*Tommy Mac*
Barry, M.S.	*Boffy and the Teacher Eater*
Baum, L.F.	*Wizard of Oz*
Bawden, N.	*Handful of Thieves*
Bawden, N.	*On the Run*
B.B.C.	*Listening and Reading*
Beresford, E.	*The Wombles*
Berg, L.	*Folk Tales*
Berna, P.	*A Hundred Million Francs*
Biegel, P.	*King of the Copper Mountain*
Blyton, E.	*The Secret Mountain*
Blyton, E.	*Five Go Off to Camp*
Blyton, E.	*The Ragamuffin Mystery*
Bond, M.	*Paddington Series*
Bond, M.	*Olga Da Polga*
Boston, L.M.	*Children of Green Knowe*
Briggs, R.	*Jim and the Beanstalk*
Brisley, J.L.	*Milly Molly Mandy*

Britton, J.	*Oxford Book of Stories for Juniors*
Buckeridge, A.	*Jennings goes to School*
Burnett, F.H.	*The Secret Garden*
Carpenter, R.	*Catweazle*
Carpenter, R.	*Catweazle and the Magic Zodiac*
Chatfield, K.	*Issi Noho*
Cleary, B.	*Ramona the Past*
Cockett, M.	*Bouncing Ball*
Collodi, C.	*Pinocchio*
Colwell, E.	*A Storytellers Choice*
Colwell, E.	*Tell Me Another Story*
Craig, W.	*Happy Endings: Stories old and new*
Cresswell, H.	*Lizzie Dripping*
Cresswell, H.	*The Piemakers*
Cresswell, H.	*Up the Pier*
Cresswell, H.	*The Gift from Winklesea*
Cunliffe, J.	*Riddles and Rhymes & Rigmaroles*
Dahl, R.	*Charlie and the Chocolate Factory*
Dahl, R.	*Charlie and the Great Glass Elevator*
Dahl, R.	*Fantastic Mr Fox*
Dahl, R.	*James and the Giant Peach*
Dahl, R.	*Danny, the Champion of the World*
Dejong, M.	*Wheel on the School*
Denesova, A.	*Fairy Tales from Japan*
Denison, M.	*Susannah of the Mounties*
Derwent, L.	*Sula*
Dickens, C.	*Oliver Twist*
Dickens, C.	*Christmas Carol*
Dickens, C.	*Christmas Stories*
Durrell, G.	*Talking Parcel*
Edwards, D.	*The Magician who kept a Pub*
Edwards, D.	*My Naughty Little Sister*
Edwards, J.E.	*Twigwidge*
Ellis, A.W.	*Old World & New World Fairy Tales*
Elstob, E.C.	*Russian Folk Tales*
Falkner, J.M.	*Moonfleet*
Fleischman, S.	*Djingo Django*
Freud, C.	*Grimble*
Gallico, P.	*Manxmouse*
Gallico, P.	*Snow Goose*
Garfield, L.	*Smith*
Garner, A.	*Weirdstone of Brisingamen*
Garner, A.	*Elidor*

Garner, A.	*The Owl Service*
Garner, A.	*Moon of Gomrath*
Garnett, E.	*Family from One End Street*
Godden, R.	*Old Woman who lived in a Vinegar Bottle*
Goodall, N.	*Donkey's Glory*
Goudge, E.	*The Little White Horse*
Grahame, K.	*The Reluctant Dragon*
Grahame, K.	*Wind in the Willows*
Green, R.L.	*Book of Dragons*
Green, R.L.	*Tales of the Greek Heroes*
Griffiths, H.	*Moshie Cat*
Grimm, J.L. and W.K.	*Fairy Tales*
Hargreaves, R.	*Mr Men Series*
Hildick, E.W.	*Lemon Kelly Series*
Hildick, E.W.	*The Questers*
Hitchcock, A.	*The Three Investigators Series*
Hoban, R.	*Good Night*
Holm, A.	*I am David*
Hope-Simpson, J.	*Book of Myths and Legends*
Hope-Simpson, J.	*Book of Witches*
Hughes, T.	*The Iron Man*
Hughes, T.	*How the Whale Became*
Hunter, N.	*Professor Branestawn*
Hunter, N.	*Homemade Dragon and Other Incredible Stories*
Hunter, N.	*Frantic Phantom*
Jansson, T.	*Finn Family Moomintroll*
Jarrell, R.	*The Animal Family*
Jones, D.W.	*Wilkins' Tooth*
Jones, D.W.	*Eight Days of Luke*
Kastner, E.	*Emil and the Detectives*
Kerr, J.	*When Hitler Stole Pink Rabbit*
King, C.	*Me and my Million*
King, C.	*Stig of the Dump*
Kingsley, C.	*The Water Babies*
Kipling, R.	*Jungle Book*
Lamb, G.F.	*Hundred Good Stories*
Lawrence, A.	*Travels of Oggy*
Lefebure, M.	*Hunting of Wilberforce Pike*
Lewis, C.S.	*The Horse and His Boy*
Lewis, C.S.	*The Magician's Nephew*
Lewis, C.S.	*Prince Caspian*
Lewis, C.S.	*The Silver Chair*
Lewis, C.S.	*The Lion, the Witch and the Wardrobe*
Lines, D.	*Run for your Life*

Lines, K.	*Greek Legends*
Lively, P.	*The Ghost of Thomas Kempe*
Loeff, A.R. Van Der	*Children on the Oregon Trail*
L'Engle, M.	*A Wrinkle in Time*
Manning, R.	*Green Smoke*
Manning, R.	*Dragon in Danger*
Manning-Sanders, R.	*A Book of Ghosts and Goblins*
Manning-Sanders, R.	*Red Indian Folk & Fairy Tales*
Marshall, J.V.	*Walkabout*
Masefield, J.	*Box of Delights*
Maupassant, G. De	*Short Stories*
Maurois, A.	*Fattypuffs and Thinifers*
Mayne, W.	*Ravensgill*
Mayne, W.	*Last Bus*
McCullagh, S.	*Griffin Pirate Stories*
Milne, A.A.	*Winnie the Pooh*
Milne, A.A.	*The House at Pooh Corner*
Montgomerie, N.	*To Read and to Tell*
Montgomery, J.	*Foxy*
Nesbit, E.	*The Railway Children*
Nesbit, E.	*The Phoenix and the Carpet*
Naughton, B.	*The Goalkeepers' Revenge*
Norton, M.	*The Borrowers*
Norton, M.	*The Borrowers Afield*
O'Brien, R.C.	*Mrs Frisby and the Rats of Nimh*
O'Brien, R.C.	*Silver Crown*
Oman, C.	*Robin Hood*
Pearce, P.	*A Dog so Small*
Pearce, P.	*Minnow on the Say*
Ponting, H.	*The Great White South*
Potter, B.	*Beatrix Potter Tales*
Power, R.	*Ten Minute Tales*
Preussler, O.	*The Little Ghost*
Preussler, O.	*The Little Witch*
Price, S.	*Devil's Piper*
Proysen, A.	*Little Old Mrs Pepperpot*
Raftery, G.	*Snow Cloud Stallion*
Ransome, A.	*Great Northern*
Ransome, A.	*Swallows & Amazons*
Regniers, B.S. and Montresor, B.	*May I Bring a Friend?*
Robinson, J.G.	*Mary, Mary*
Rodgers, M.	*Freaky Friday*

Rodari, G.	*The Pie in the Sky*
Serraillier, I.	*The Silver Sword*
Serraillier, I.	*There's No Escape*
Sherlock, P.	*West Indian Folk Tales*
Sissons, R.A.	*Escape from the Dark*
Sleigh, B.	*Carbonel*
Smith, D.	*Hundred and One Dalmatians*
Spyri, J.	*Heidi*
Storr, C.	*Lucy Runs Away*
Swift, J.	*Gulliver's Travels*
Szudek, A.	*Amber Mountain*
Tibber, R.	*Aristide*
Todd, B.E.	*Worzel Gummidge*
Todd, H.E.	*Bobby Brewster*
Tolkien, J.R.	*The Hobbit*
Tolkien, J.R.	*Farmer Giles of Ham*
Townsend, J.R.	*Pirate's Island*
Townsend, J.R.	*Gumbles Yard*
Trease, G.	*Cue for Treason*
Trease, G.	*Bows against the Barons*
Treece, H.	*Viking's Dawn*
Treece, H.	*The Dreamtime*
Turnbull, A.S.	*George*
Twain, M.	*Adventures of Tom Sawyer*
Unstead, R.J.	*The Story of Britain*
Verne, J.	*Twenty Thousand Leagues under the Sea*
Wakefield, S.	*Bottersnikes and Gumbles*
White, E.B.	*Charlotte's Web*
Wilder, L.I.	*Little House in the Big Woods*
Williams, J. and Abrashkin, R.	*Danny Dunn, Time Traveller*
Williams, U.M.	*Adventures of the Little Wooden Horse*
Williams, U.M.	*Gobbolino the Witch's Cat*
Williamson, H.	*Tarka the Otter*

Full list of 'themes' or topics mentioned by junior teachers as being already studied, in progress or planned for 1976/77. (Extension of Table 18).

Adaptation
Adjectives
Advent
Advertising
Africa
Air
Aircraft
Air Pressure
America
Amphibians
Ancient Egypt
Angles
Animals
Annual Events
Antarctic
Ants
Arctic
Area
Asia
Australia
Austria
Autumn
Aztecs

Balance
Ball games
Basford-it's growth
Battles and Weapons
Beasts of Prey
Beds

Brunei
Buildings
Butterflies
Bees
Beverages
Bible Themes
Bicycles
Birds
Blacksmiths
Body
Bones
Bonfire night
Books
Bottles
Breakfast
Bridges
British history
British industries
British Isles
British wild animals
Bronze Age

Calendar
Camping
Canada
Canals
Caribbean Isles
Cars
Castles
Caterpillars

Cats
Cavemen
Cavemen to Vikings
Caves
Change
'Charlie and the Chocolate Factory'
Children of other lands
Chimney sweeps
China
Christ as a healer
Christians
Christmas
Churches
Circles
Circuses
Civil war
Clay
Clifton estate
Climates
Clocks and cogs
Clothing and costumes
Clowns
Coal
Cocoa
Cold
Cold regions
Colours
Columbus
Common market countries
Commonwealth
Communications
Communities
Conkers
Conservation
Containers
Continental customs
Copper Mountains
Costume (historical)
Countries
Countryside
Cowboys and indians
Craftsmen
Creation
Creatures great and small
Crops of the world
Crusades
Crystals
Cultures

Dairy farming
Danger
Darkness
Days and nights
Decimals
Decorations
Demolition
Deprived children
Derbyshire
Deserts
Development of man
Diets and health
Dinosaurs
Disappearing animals
Disasters
Discovery
Donkey sanctuary
Dragons
Dreams
Drought
Dustmen

Early man
Early history
Earth
Earthquakes
Easter
East Midlands
Edward VI
Edwardian Europe
Egyptians
Electricity
Elizabethan England
Enchanted forest
Energy
Engines and motivation
England
Entertainment
Environmental study
Eskimoes
Europe
Evolution of man
Experiments
Explorers

Fabrics and textiles
Fairy tales
Families

Famous painters
Famous people
Famous saints
Fantastic creatures
Faraway places
Far East
Farmers year
Farms
Feudal system
Field study
Fire
Firsts (records/inventions)
First aid
Five senses
Fish
Fishing
Flags and emblems
Flight
Flowers
Flying
Food
Food and animals
Food and drink
Foreign countries
Forgiveness
Fossils
Foxes
Fractions
France
French revolution
Fruit
Fruit and vegetables
Fuel
Fungi
Furniture and clothing

Games and sport
Garden
Gedling and Nottingham
Germs
Georgian England
'Geography topics'
Geology
Ghosts in Nottingham
Ghost stories
Giants
Glass
Go-carts

Goose Fair
Graphs
Greece
Greek gods
Groups
Growing things
Growing up
Gunthorpe
Guy Fawkes
Gypsies

Hallowe'en
Hands
Hands and feet
Harvest
Hats
Health
Heat
The Heavens
Hedgerow
Henry VIII and wives
Hibernation
History around you
History of Nottingham
'History topics'
Hobbies
Holes
Holland
Holidays
Homes
Honey bees
Horses
Hostelling
Hot and cold
Houdini
Houses
How life began
How the days got their names
How we got our names
How we used to live
How we went on holiday
How, who, where and when
Hygiene

Ice and snow
Iceland
Important dates
Important people

Indians
Industrial archaeology
Industrial Revolution
Insects
In the woods
Invasion of Britain
Inventions
Inventors
Investigation corner
Ireland
Iron and steel
Islands
Italy

Jamaica
Japan
Jesus — his life and time
Jobs
Joseph (bible)
Jubilee
Jungle book
Jungles

Kibbutz
King Arthur
Kings and queens
Kites
Knights and castles

Lake district
Land usage and reclamation
'Language topics'
Law and order
Legends
Light
Like and unlike
Lincoln
Literacy
Lives
Living in the community
Livingstone
Living things
Local environment
Local geography
Locked doors
Locomotion
London
London's poor

Looking after yourself

Machines
Magic and mystery
Magnets
Major invasions
Mammals
Man (development)
Man's world
Maps
Markets and fairs
Mary Queen of Scots
Masks
Mass media
Materials
Measuring
Medicine
Medieval times
Mediterranean sea
Mexico
Middle Ages
Migration
Milk
Minerals
Miners
Mini-beasts
Mirror images
Missionaries
Monarchs
Money
Monsters
Moses
Mountains
Movement
Moving around
Music
Musical instruments

Names
National parks
Nativity
Natural resources
Nature study
Needs of living things
News
Newspapers
New Testament
New Zealand

Night
Noah's Ark
Norman Conquest
Normans
Nottingham
Numbers
Nurses and hospitals

Oceans
Oil and North Sea gas
Old Testament
Oliver (musical)
Opposites
Orchestra
Other countries
Our area
Our class and school
Our city
Our living world
Our school
Ourselves
Owls

Pacific Ocean
Palestine
Pancake day
Paper
Patron saints
Patterns
Patterns in building
People
People at work
People here
People in the Bible
People in the past
People of other lands
People on whom we depend
People there
People who help us
Peter Pan
Pets
Pied Piper
Pioneers
Pirates
Places to live
Planets
Plants
Plastics

Playhouse
Polar regions
Police
Pollution
Pompeii
Pond life
Poppy Day
Post Office
Pottery
Power
Prehistoric animals
Prehistoric Britain
Printing
Puppetry

'Railway Children'
Railways
Rainbow colours
Rebellions
Red Indians
Religious education
Reptiles
Resuscitation
Research skills
Restoration England
Rivers and canals
Roads
Road safety
Robin Hood
Rocks
Roman Britain
Romans
Roots and vegetables
Royal family
Rubber
Rubbish
Rudders and wings
Ruth (Bible)

Safety in the home
Sailors and ships
Saint Francis
Salvation Army
Scarecrow
'Science topics'
School
School field
Scotland

Sea
Seadogs
Seasons
Seasonal events
Seeds
Senses
September
Settlers
Shape and size
Shapes
Shelters
Shining things
Ships
Shire horses
Shopping survey
Shops
Signs and symbols
Simon Peter (Bible)
Small animals
Snakes
Snow White
Social development of the working man
Sound
Space
Spain
Speed
Spiders
Spirals
Sport
Spots
Spring
Stamps
Steam
Steam trains
Stone age
Street maps
Streets
Stress and strain
Strong and weak
Structures
Stories
Stuarts
Summer camp
Summer holidays
Sun
Superstitions
Surveys
Survival

Switzerland
Symmetry

Teeth
Television
Television characters
Temperature
Tessellations
That's strange!
Then and now
Things which live in holes
Thinking
Timber
Time
Topical events
Tower of London
Toys (science)
Tracks and pathways
Trades and crafts
Traffic survey
Transport
Travel
Trees
Trent (river)
Triangles
Tubes and cylinders
Tudors
Tudors and Stuarts
Twentieth century Britain

Urban wildlife
Underground creatures
Underground people
Underwater
Union Jack
Unions
United Kingdom
Universe

Victorian children and their toys
Victorians
Vikings
Village study
Volcanoes
'Voyage of the Griffin'

War
Water

Water conservation
Water mills
Water safety
Water travel
Water and water power
Weapons
Weather
Weaving
Weight
West Indies
Whales
What shall I be?
Wheels
Where things come from
Where we live
Wild life
Wind
Wings
Winter
Witches
Wollaton canal
Wollaton Park
Wood
Work and play
World
World War 1
Worms

You and your environment

Zoo

Full list of topics or interests mentioned by infant teachers as being already studied, in progress, or planned, for 1976/7.

Adult occupations
Air
'All things bright and beautiful'
America
Animals
Arctic
Australia
Autumn

Bags
Balance
Ballet
Batman
Bears
Bees
Bells
Big and little
Birds
Black
Black and white
Blue
Boats
Body
Bones and skeletons
Bonfire night
Bottles
Bravery
Bread
Brown
Brushes
Bulbs

Buildings
Butterflies

Calendar
Capacity
Cars
Castles
Caterpillars
Cats
Cavemen
Change
'Charlie and the Chocolate
  Factory'
Children's games
Children from other lands
Christmas
Churches
'Cinderella'
Circles
Circus
Clay
Clocks
Clothes
Crafts
Coal
Coats
Cold countries
Collections
Colours
Cooking
Countries

Cowboys

'David the Shepherd Boy'
Days of the week
Dinosaurs
Doctors and nurses
Dogs
Dragons
Drought
Ducks

Easter
Eggs
Electricity
Entertainment
Environment
Eskimoes
Explorers
Europe

Faces
Fairy Stories
Families
Famous people
Farms
Favourite stories
Favourite television programmes
Favourite things
Feathers
Feeling things
Feet
Fire
'Fire Bird'
Firemen
Fireworks
Fishing
Flight
Floating
Flowers
Food
Football
Four
France
Frost
Fruit

Ghosts and spooks
Giants

Glass
Glitter and shine
'Gobbolino'
Going to hospital
Gold
'Goldilocks and the
    Three Bears'
Goose Fair
Graphs
Green
Growth
Guinea pigs
Guy Fawkes

Hair
Hallowe'en
Hands
'Hansel and Gretel'
Harvest festival
Hats
Health
Hearing
Heavy and light
Hibernation
Holes and cavities
Holidays
Holland
Homes
Horns
Horses
Hospital
Hot and cold
Houses
How to keep ourselves clean
Human body
'Humpty Dumpty'

Icebergs
Indians
Insects

'Jack and the Beanstalk'
Jesus
Jewellery
Jubilee
Jungle

Keeping warm

Kitchen
King Kong
Kings and queens
Knights

Ladybirds
Large and small
Legs
Length
Letters
Light
Light and heavy
Lighthouses
Likes and dislikes
Lines
Little things
London

Magic
'Magic Roundabout'
Magnetism
Man in space
Manners
Market
Mass
May Day
Measuring
Mending the road
Mermaids
Metals
Migration
Model town
Money
Monkeys
Monsters
Months
Moths
Mother's Day
Mouse
Moving
'Mr Men'
Mums
Music
Musical instruments
My day
My home
Myself

Nativity
Nature
Neighbours
News
Newspapers
Night
Night and day
Noah's Ark
Nocturnal animals
Noise
Nomads
North America
North Pole
Norway
Nottingham
Numbers
'Nutcracker Suite'

Objects brought by children
Odd and even
On the road
One
Opposites
Orange
Ourselves
Outings

Pairs
Pancake Day
Pantomimes
Paper
Parks
Patterns
Penguins
People
People at work
People outside the
  community
People that help us
People we see
'Peter Pan'
'Peter and the Wolf'
Pets
'Pied Piper of Hamblin'
Pink
'Pinnochio'
Pirates
Plants

Plastic
Polar bears
Police
Pond life
Post office
Postmen
Poultry
Prehistoric animals

Queen Elizabeth
Queens

Rabbits
Rain
Red
Red Indians
'Red Riding Hood'
Red, white and blue
Reflections
Reptiles
Reservoirs
Roads
Road safety
'Robin Hood'
Robots
Rocks
Romans
Rope and string
Rough and smooth
Round
Round and about
Royal family
Rubber
Rufford Park

St. David's Day
Salt
Santa Claus
Scotland
Sea
Seaside
Seasons
Seeds
Senses
Sets
Shapes
Shells
Shiny things

Ships
Shipwreck
Shoes
Shops
Sir Francis Drake
'Sleeping Beauty'
Smell
Snow
'Snow Queen'
'Snow White'
'Sorcerer's Apprentice'
Space
Space travel
Sparkling
Spiders
Sport
Spring
Spring flowers
Squares
Stone age
String
Summer
Sun and moon
Supermarkets
Swans
Swimming
Symmetry

Tall and short
Teeth
Television
Texture
Theatre
'The Hobbit'
'The Ugly Duckling'
Things that I like
Things that go round
Things that make me laugh
'Three Little Pigs'
Time
Touch
Town
Toys
Toyshop
Traffic
Trains
Transport
Travel

Treasures from the Earth
Trees
Twelve
Two

Underground
Under the sea
Under water
Uniforms
Union Jack
United States of America

Vikings
Village
'Village with Three Corners'
Volcanoes
Volume

Watches
Water
Water transport
Weather
Weddings
Weighing
Wendy House
Wet and dry
Where we live
Whales
Wheels
When I grow up
White
Wild animals
Windmills
'Winnie the Pooh'
Winter
Witches
'Wizard of Oz'
Wizards
Wollaton
Wood
Wooden things

Yellow

Zoos

Appendix IV

Membership of the Advisory Committee

Mr F Cummings, NAS/UWT representative
Miss J. M. Eyre, NAHT representative
Mr T. W. B. Gregory, Educational Adviser, Notts. County Council
Mrs P. Marshall, Assistant Director of Education, Notts. County Council
Mr W. Middlebrook, Dean, School of Education, Trent Polytechnic
  (Chairman)
Mr J. B. Neilson, Deputy Director, Trent Polytechnic
Mr D. H. Smith, NUT representative
Mr R. R. Ward, Area Education Officer for Gedling and then Nottingham
Dr M. Bassey, Reader, School of Education, Trent Polytechnic

Research officers

Maureen Barratt
Sally Baxter
Dorothy Beach
Veronica Briston
Barbara Calvert
Margaret Caurton
Annira Cutts
Williamina Davis
Catherine Dewar
Janet Edwards
Janice Every
Susan Godfrey
Susan Greaves
Nina Hatch
Judith Hewitt
Lois Hill
Sue Hill
Belinder Humble
Pamela Ingram
Maisie Johnson
Patricia Kelley
Kerpal Lehal
Lynn Marlow
Valerie Moyes
Jennifer Rushton
Joy Anne Saxton
Martin Sweet
Olive Taylor
Janet Terry
Eileen Toone
Lorna Wheatcroft